ALIVE BENEATH THE ASHES

Finding the fire Within

& Reclaiming Your True self

By

DR. SAIF QAZI

For permissions and inquiries, contact:
✉ hello@drsaifqazi.in

First edition published in 2025
ISBN: 9789334295009

Author's Declaration & Disclaimer

This is an original work by the author. All concepts, reflections, and stories are either personal interpretations, fictionalised illustrations, or synthesised from scientific and publicly available sources. Any resemblance to real persons is coincidental unless stated.

This book is intended for educational and personal growth purposes only. It is not a substitute for professional medical, psychological, or therapeutic advice. Readers are advised to consult qualified professionals for health or mental wellness concerns.

www.drsaifqazi.in
Mirror Verse Publishing

✿ *Brains Behind the Book*

Gratitude to the Hearts and Minds That Shaped This Journey

Research & Contribution

- **Dr. Narayan Patil, MD (Ayu)**
  Principal, RJS Medical College, Kopargaon
- **Dr. Major Jeetendra Singh**
  Professor & HOD, Pharmacology
  GMC & MPGIMER, MUHS Nashik
- **Dr. Amit Tak, MD (Psychiatrist)**
- **Dr. Suhail Makhdumi, MD (Physiology)**
  Lecturer IIMSR Jalna
- **Dr. Vishal Ingle**
  Police Inspector, BHMS, LLB, LLM, PGD Forensics, PGDCL, PGDHAM
- **Dr Hadi**
  BHMS M.Sc. (Pharma Med)

Editorial Team

- Dr. Bajrang Avasthi & Dr Sayyed Irfan Ali

Cover & Interior Design

Asif Shaikh & Dr. Saif Qazi

Proofreading

- Zeenat Qazi & Sajeda Qazi

Special Thanks

To **Dr. B.S.V. Prasad**, renowned psychiatrist,
for your clinical insights in psychiatry and for healing me when I needed it most.

This book is not mine alone. It's a shared pulse, a collective breath.

Dedication

To the ones who stayed soft
in a world that rewards only sharp edges.
To those who healed quietly,
rebuilt slowly,
and kept going without needing to be seen.

This is for you.
You were never broken only becoming.

And to my sons, **Tabish and Faiz**
Everything I unlearned, everything I reclaimed,
was so you could grow up freer than I did.
You are the reason my heart stayed open.

Preface

An Invitation Back to Yourself

Dear Reader,

If you're holding this book, it means one thing:

Some part of you is still alive beneath the noise.

Still reaching.

Still remembering.

This book isn't here to teach you how to be better.

It's here to help you come home.

Home to the version of you that existed before survival, success, and self-editing buried your reflection.

You are not broken.

You are not lost.

You are right on time.

Each chapter ahead is not a prescription.

It's a conversation—between the soul you silenced and the self you are ready to remeet.

You won't be asked to hustle, strive, or perform here.

You'll be asked to soften.

To listen.

To stay.

Healing is not a race.

It's not a reinvention.

It's a return.

And you are already walking it—one quiet, stubborn, beautiful step at a time.

Welcome back.

With quiet faith in your unfolding,

Dr. Saif Qazi

Foreword

by Dr. B.S.V. Prasad
Associate Professor & Senior Psychiatrist, Nashik

Every now and then, someone walks into your clinic and leaves a lasting impression, not just because of what they're going through, but because of how they choose to face it.

Dr. Saif Qazi was one of those people.

When we first met, he came not just as a doctor, but as someone quietly seeking clarity, wanting to understand his own emotional world more deeply. There was no rush, no drama only sincerity and a willingness to do the work. That honesty stood out.

What began as a personal search soon turned into something much more meaningful. Over time, I saw him approach his healing with the same thoughtfulness and discipline he brings to his medical practice. He didn't just want to feel better—he wanted to grow, to understand, and eventually, to give back.

This book is a reflection of that journey.

Alive Beneath the Ashes is not written from a distance. It comes from someone who has walked through the difficult questions and come out with a deeper sense of self—and a desire to help others do the same. The book blends science with real experience, but more than anything, it carries warmth.

It's rare to see someone transform their personal pain into something that can guide and support others. Saif has done that—with grace, humility, and a quiet strength.

I had the privilege of witnessing this journey closely. And I feel just as privileged to write these few words as he shares his story with the world.

Dr. B.S.V. Prasad
Associate Professor & Senior Consultant Psychiatrist,
Nashik
April 2025

TABLE OF CONTENTS

PART ONE

THE GHOSTS, YOU DIDN'T KNOW YOU WERE CARRYING

PART TWO

THE SILENT ARCHITECTS OF YOUR SURVIVAL

PART THREE

LEARNING A NEW WAY TO BREATHE

PART FOUR

BECOMING YOUR OWN SANCTUARY

Introduction: A Book That Returns You to Yourself

You're not broken. You're encoded. This book doesn't fix you; it helps you finally hear yourself again.

You didn't find this book. It found you. Not to make you better, but to bring you back. Back to the version of you that was never missing, only muted.

You've tried the checklists. You've swallowed the affirmations. You've sprinted through self-help like it was a race to worthiness. But the ache never left.

Because what you've been searching for was never a new version of you. It was a way to come home — to the one you buried beneath survival, success, and self-editing.

This book doesn't offer steps. It offers safety. It won't hand you another strategy to perform.

It will hold up a mirror — so precise, so honest — you won't be able to lie to yourself anymore.

You won't just read this book. You'll feel it.
Because this isn't self-help.
It's a return to what was always yours—but temporarily forgotten.
And you're exactly on time.

Before We Begin: Why This Isn't Just Another Self-Help Book

Most self-help books tell you how to become someone else. This one helps you remember who you were before you forgot.

There are no bullet-pointed breakthroughs here.

No fixes. No frameworks.

Just quiet recognitions that lead you back to yourself.

You're a soul that's been trying to feel safe enough to return home.

Reprogram whispered the truth.

This one holds it steady until you can believe it.

You won't find hype, hustle, or hollow motivation here.

What you'll find is safety.

Language that slows you down.

Ideas that soothe before they spark.

Practices that don't demand more of you — they help you release what was never yours.

This book began its journey as *Reprogram*, a poetic exploration of identity, healing, and transformation.

Its emotional intensity struck a deep chord, especially among seekers looking for meaning beneath the noise of modern life.

But something was missing for those who needed more clarity, more structure, more science.

For readers who didn't want metaphors — they wanted mechanisms.

This new edition is for them.

We've retained the soul of the original but restructured its spine.

The emotional truths are now woven through with neuroscience, cultural wisdom, and practical strategies.

Every idea that once floated like poetry now lands like a blueprint.

You'll still find echoes of the original.

The longing.

The honesty.

The fire.

But here, they're sharpened into tools.

This is not a rewrite.

It's a reinvention.

It's *Reprogram* — rewired.

Why This Book Exists

Most books tell you how to become more—this one helps you remember what you've always been.

You won't find generic advice or productivity hacks here. Instead, you'll find patterns, proofs, and practices that decode the invisible scripts you've inherited.

We'll explore how trauma shapes your nervous system, how early rewards hardwire your habits, and how healing happens—not just in the mind, but in the body.

This isn't a book about adding more.
It's about subtracting the noise.
It's about returning to the version of you that always existed—beneath performance, perfectionism, and borrowed expectations.

If you're tired of being told who to be,
This book will help you remember who you were before you forgot.

❁ About the Practices You'll Find in This Book

A Gentle Note Before You Begin Chapter One

Throughout this book, you'll come across short, optional sections called **Science Soothing**.
These are not rituals.
They are not spiritual obligations.
They do not belong to any religious tradition.
And they will never ask you to do anything that feels uncomfortable or unfamiliar.

Each of these practices is grounded in neuroscience, somatic safety, and emotional psychology.
They are designed to gently support your healing — by calming your nervous system, reprogramming old emotional patterns, and creating a sense of safety inside your own body.

You are never required to do them. They are simply invitations — quiet doorways you may choose to open if they resonate with you.

We understand that healing is deeply personal.
This book honours every background, every faith, and every path.

Whether you read this as a Muslim, Hindu, Christian, Sikh, agnostic, spiritual seeker, or someone who doesn't identify with any label — these practices are for *humans*, not belief systems.

They do not ask you to abandon your values.
They simply offer you a chance to feel more at home within yourself. If something doesn't feel right for you,

you're free to skip it.
You are always in charge.

Healing isn't about control.
It's about safety, clarity, and quiet return.

These practices are here for one reason only —
To remind your nervous system that peace is possible.

And you are safe to begin.
— *Dr. Saif Qazi*

PART ONE

The Ghosts, You Didn't Know You Were Carrying

CHAPTER

1

The Ghost in Your Mind – Inherited, Installed, Invisible

"What you call your personality might just be your past, rehearsing itself." — Dr. Saif Qazi

Some ghosts don't haunt you from outside—they speak from within. Not in screams or shadows, but in thoughts that feel like your own voice. "Don't say too much." "Don't trust too easily." "Don't take up too much space." You believe it's your personality. But it's not. It's your past rehearsing itself.

Healing doesn't begin when you change who you are. It begins when you question who taught you to be this way.

The Room, You Didn't Know You Lived In

Imagine waking up in a home you've lived in for years. You know every corner. Every creaking board. But one day, you find a door you've never seen. Behind it is a room filled with whispers—not yours, but of others: caretakers, cultures, classrooms. These voices don't shout. They repeat. Softly. Endlessly. So you mistake them for truth.

This hidden room is your subconscious—the quiet basement of the mind, formed when your brain was still under construction.

In childhood, your brain absorbs beliefs like wet cement—soft, impressionable. Between ages 0–7, your mind operates primarily in **theta waves**, a dreamlike state where boundaries between self and environment blur. That means much of what you now call "you" was never chosen by you.

It was installed.

"Until you make the unconscious conscious, it will direct your life and you will call it fate."

— Carl Gustav Jung

This is why so many of your traits, reactions, and patterns feel automatic. You didn't consciously choose them. Your nervous system simply rehearsed them into identity.

The Neuroscience of Inherited Thought

You weren't born afraid to speak. Or doubt yourself. Or apologise for your needs. You learned these patterns from repetition—your nervous system coding safety in survival, not in authenticity.

Studies show that children raised in environments with unpredictable emotional responses often develop hypervigilant nervous systems. Their **amygdala**, the brain's threat detector, becomes overactive. The **prefrontal cortex**, responsible for reflection and choice, takes a back seat.

"If you feel unsafe being yourself, your biology will adjust to keep you liked, not real."

In simple words: You don't choose self-silencing. Your biology defaults to it—until you interrupt the loop.

Echo Story: Karan and the Ghost of "Be Careful"

Karan, 32, grew up in a home where his mother always said, "Don't take risks. Play safe." Her voice was full of love—but also of fear. When he turned down a scholarship to study abroad because it felt "too uncertain," he thought it was logic. But later, in therapy, he realised: it was the ghost of her anxiety, living in his decisions.

He wasn't resisting opportunity. He was obeying inherited alarm systems.

Once he saw that, something shifted. The next time he felt fear about a bold choice, he asked himself: "Is this my fear—or someone else's inheritance?" He made the call anyway. Just to see what would happen. And in that small act, he began rewriting the script.

That single question became his key.

Practice: Ghost-Spotting

Start by listening. For one week, gently observe the recurring thoughts that govern your behaviour. Place your hand on the part of your body where the ghost tends to speak—your throat, chest, or stomach—and breathe into that space as you write.

Write down:

- One belief about your voice
- One belief about your worth
- One belief about your limits
- One place in your body where you feel that belief live

Then ask yourself: **Where did I first hear this?**

If it wasn't you—then it doesn't belong to you. You inherited it. And what's inherited… can be examined. Felt. And eventually, rewritten.

"Inherited doesn't mean destined. Awareness is your exit."

Cultural Reflection: Indian Conditioning

In many Indian homes, silence is mistaken for respect. Obedience is mistaken for virtue. Children are told, "Don't answer back," "Don't ask why," "Good kids don't complain."

So, they don't.

But as adults, they carry that silence like a second skin—afraid to express, to say no, to disagree. Not because they're weak, but because their nervous system still believes disagreement equals danger.

'What was called 'good behaviour' was often just fear in polite disguise.

Your healing does not dishonour your upbringing. It dignifies it—by ensuring the patterns that came from pain, end with you.

Final Whisper

You don't need to burn your past. You only need to see it clearly. Your ghosts aren't villains. They're messengers. Outdated protectors. Misunderstood guardians. Invite them to speak, then update the story they forgot to finish. Once you name the ghost, it loses its power.

You were never broken. You were programmed. The room that once echoed with others' fears can now begin to echo with your own voice. And anything programmed… can be rewritten.

"You cannot outgrow what you haven't out named."

Sacred Reflection

What thought feels like yours—but might actually be inherited?

❁ Bonus Practice: Science Soothing

Ghost-Spotting — A Gentle Inquiry

If today's reflection stirred something inside you, try this soft practice:

Step 1: Listen for the ghosts.
For one week, gently observe the recurring thoughts that govern your behaviour.

Step 2: Place your hand on the part of your body where this ghost tends to speak — your throat, chest, or stomach. Breathe slowly into that space.

Step 3: Write down...
- One belief about your voice
- One belief about your worth
- One belief about your limits
- One place in your body where this belief lives

Step 4: Ask yourself:
Where did I first hear this? Whose voice is this?

If it wasn't you — then it doesn't belong to you.

Inherited doesn't mean destined. Awareness is your exit.

Why This Practice Works

These small practices may seem simple — but they speak directly to your nervous system.

When you place a hand on your heart, breathe slowly, or name a new truth, you activate the **parasympathetic nervous system** and **vagus nerve**, both of which calm the amygdala and reduce cortisol — your body's primary stress hormone.

Repeated acts of safety send your brain new signals, helping it **rewire emotional memory networks** through a process called **neuroplasticity**.

Over time, these micro-moments reshape how your nervous system responds to the world.

You don't need to force healing.

You just need to offer your body a new experience — gently, consistently.

CHAPTER

2

Emotional Inheritance – What Wasn't Yours, But Lives in You

"Some of the weight you carry was never meant to be yours. It was handed to you by people who didn't know how to put it down." — *Dr. Saif Qazi*

There are behaviours you don't understand in yourself. Fears that feel out of proportion. Reactions that arrive before reason. You may think, *This is just who I am.* But what if it isn't?

What if you're living with emotions that were never processed—because they were never yours to begin with?

What Emotional Inheritance Looks Like

Three Signs Your Emotion Might Be Inherited:

- Your reaction feels bigger than the situation.
- You don't know why you're triggered—but it's familiar.
- You feel guilt, panic, or shame for simply existing as yourself.

How It Shows Up in Modern Life:

- Struggling to receive praise or success.
- Repeating relationship patterns despite wanting different.
- Feeling unsafe in visibility or leadership.
- Anxiety in spending, resting, or saying no.

You might find yourself flinching when praised. Or rushing to apologise when no one's upset. Or choosing emotional hunger over the risk of disappointment. These responses weren't born in you. They were passed down—transferred not just through stories, but through tone, silence, facial expressions, and nervous systems.

You didn't just inherit your grandmother's eyes or your father's height. You inherited their fear. Their tension. Their blueprint for survival.

In homes where no one talked about emotions, children became fluent in reading moods instead. A slammed door, a held breath, an unspoken grudge—all became cues for how to behave. This is emotional inheritance: learning who you must be in order to be safe.

"Emotional austerity is passed down in silences louder than words."

"Children don't just learn language from their environment. They learn what is allowed to feel, show, or hide."

The Neuroscience of Inherited Emotion

"Trauma decontextualized in a family over time can look like personality."

— Resmaa Menakem

Neuroscience confirms what ancient cultures intuited: unprocessed trauma doesn't just vanish—it transmits. Studies from Mount Sinai and AIIMS-ICMR show that trauma alters not just the brain, but gene expression. Through a process called **epigenetic tagging**, emotional environments change how genes are activated without changing DNA itself. A landmark 2015 study from Mount Sinai showed that children and grandchildren of Holocaust survivors had higher stress hormone expression—suggesting trauma rewires biology for generations. This means a parent's unresolved anxiety can influence how a child's stress circuits are wired.

You might be reacting not to the present, but to echoes of past generations—ghost frequencies your body's radio never learned to turn off.

"You are not starting from scratch. You are starting from history."

Echo Story: Neha and the Panic That Wasn't Hers

Neha, a 28-year-old law student, kept having panic attacks during oral arguments. She had never faced trauma directly—but every time she stood up to speak, her body froze.

During a therapy session, she remembered how her mother, a teacher, was humiliated publicly by a school principal. "They made her cry in front of a whole assembly," she said. Neha had only been six. But her body remembered. Her throat remembered. Her nervous system had tagged *visibility* as unsafe.

When she finally traced the feeling back, she realised: this wasn't her fear. It was an inheritance. Her healing began not by forcing confidence, but by gently whispering, "This isn't mine, but I can choose something new."

Cultural Reflection: The Stories We Were Told

In many Indian families, emotional inheritance is disguised as tradition:

"Boys don't cry."

- "Keep your problems inside the home."
- "Don't question your elders."

So we perform instead of process. We endure instead of express. And we confuse emotional austerity for strength.

But healing means untangling respect from silence, and love from self-erasure. It means realising that our parents' pain doesn't have to become our personality.

"What was sacred for survival can be updated for belonging."

Generational Mantra

"I honour your survival by choosing beyond it."

Final Whisper

You don't heal by rejecting your ancestors. You heal by facing what they couldn't, feeling what they couldn't name, and choosing what they never had the safety to imagine.

You carry their strength—but you are not required to carry their suffering.

"The burden ends where the awareness begins."

Sacred Reflection

Think of one emotion you carry often. Now ask: When did this first arrive—and was it ever truly mine?

✿ Bonus Practice: Science Soothing

Spot – Trace – Disrupt – Anchor

If an emotional reaction feels louder than the moment — it might be older than you think.

✦Step 1: Spot

Notice a recurring response — panic, withdrawal, over-apology. Ask gently: *"Does this feel bigger than the moment?"*

✦Step 2: Trace

Close your eyes and recall the earliest memory or family pattern where this emotion first made sense.
Whose survival script are you still carrying?

✦Step 3: Disrupt

Place a hand on the part of your body where this emotion lives — your gut, chest, or jaw.
Breathe.
Say gently: *"This belongs to the past."*

✦Step 4: Anchor

Choose one small, repeatable act that contradicts the old code:

Holding eye contact.

Saying, "I'm proud of this."

Resting without guilt.

Receiving a compliment without deflecting.

Pausing before apologising.

Each act is a neural rebellion. A new pattern being born.

💭 *"Inherited doesn't mean permanent. It means editable."*

Why This Practice Works

Trauma-based patterns live in both memory and muscle.
Using **touch, breath, and naming** calms the amygdala and activates the **vagus nerve**, signalling safety.
With repetition, these inputs rewire emotional reflexes through **neuroplasticity** — turning survival habits into conscious choice.

By tracing emotional origins, you engage the **prefrontal cortex**, restoring reflection where reaction once ruled. Anchoring a new behaviour creates a **counter-memory** — a lived experience that begins to replace the inherited script.

CHAPTER

3

Generational Loops – Why You Repeat What You Swore You Wouldn't

"You swore you'd never become them. But here you are—with their fear in your breath, their caution in your spine, their sadness echoing in your laughter." — Dr. Saif Qazi

You look at your parents—or their shadows—and vow, *Not me. I'll be different.* But somehow, you catch yourself speaking the same lines. Using the same silences. Enacting the very behaviours that once hurt you.
Why?
Because what you mentally reject, your nervous system may still repeat. Not by choice. By encoding.

What Are Generational Loops?

Generational loops are emotional patterns passed down not by decision, but by repetition. They're the rules you absorbed by observing, not being taught. The patterns you swore to avoid—but now find stitched into your instincts.

"Your body doesn't speak logic. It speaks memory."

If your mother softened every conflict into silence, you might struggle to speak your truth. If your father equated success with self-neglect, you may fear rest. These are not personality flaws. They are inherited programs.

Loops aren't just behaviours. They're emotional strategies passed across time:

- Avoiding intimacy because love once meant loss.
- Over-working because rest was punished.
- People-pleasing because boundaries once led to abandonment.

"The repetition of trauma becomes encoded in the body, not as a memory, but as a response."

— Peter Levine (Trauma expert and founder of Somatic Experiencing)

And because the body remembers, it becomes your default.

The Neuroscience of Repetition

Neuroscience shows that the brain builds neural pathways based on what is repeated, not what is true. This means that repeated emotional experiences—shame, rejection, instability—become stronger than conscious intentions.

A 2019 study from the University of Michigan found that adults who experienced emotionally unpredictable parenting showed greater amygdala activation even in safe environments. Their bodies could not relax—not because of present danger, but because of historic inconsistency.

"You're not broken. You're following a loop wired into you for protection."

Echo Story: Ayaan and the Scar of Being "Too Much"

Ayaan, a 34-year-old writer, had always been told, "You're too emotional." So he became measured. Restrained. Acceptable. But inside, he boiled.

His relationships suffered—people called him detached. He was praised for being composed but felt chronically unseen.

In therapy, he remembered childhood dinners where his joy was shushed. His tears punished. His aliveness… inconvenient.

That's when he saw it: he had looped himself into invisibility. Not because he wanted to—but because his nervous system equated emotion with exile.

His healing began with contradiction. He cried aloud. Laughed without editing. Felt rage and didn't apologise. He wasn't seeking rebellion. He was seeking return.

Cultural Reflection: Loops Within Indian Families

In many Indian households, loops are mistaken for values:

- Sacrifice = love.
- Silence = strength.
- Endurance = identity.

So when you begin to rest, speak up, or say no—you may feel guilt not because you're wrong, but because you're rewriting the script.

Some loops began in scarcity. Others in shame. Many in colonial or caste-coded trauma. But if they continue through you, they can also end through you.

"The most radical thing you can do in some families… is feel safely."

Generational Mantra

"They passed down fear as love. I return it as clarity."

Final Whisper

You're not failing by becoming different. You're fulfilling what they couldn't finish. Loops are not destiny. They are invitations.

And every time you pause, breathe, and choose a gentler response—

You are not betraying your lineage.

You are completing it.

Sacred Reflection

What emotional pattern do you repeat—not because it fits, but because it's familiar? What would happen if you chose differently,

even once?

✿ Bonus Practice: Science Soothing

Break the Loop – A New Rhythm for the Nervous System

Patterns don't only live in memory; they take shelter in your daily movements—how you pause, how you react, how you brace. The loop often begins without your permission, but you can begin to rewrite it with gentle precision.

✦ Identify the pattern: Begin by noticing one recurring behaviour that tends to appear when you're under emotional stress. Perhaps you shut down during conflict, apologise excessively, overthink a simple interaction, or bury yourself in overwork. This reaction may feel like second nature, but it often points to something older and unspoken.

✦ Trace the loop: Reflect quietly. Ask yourself, "When did I first feel the need to act this way?" Whose voice shaped this reaction—was it a parent's silence, a teacher's disapproval, a cultural script you never questioned? Identifying the source softens the grip it holds over you.

✦ Disrupt the pathway: In the moment you catch the pattern, pause. Place your hand over your sternum or jaw—areas where emotional memory often resides. Breathe deeply into that space and say gently, "I choose a new way." This physical cue begins to separate the present from the past, and tells your nervous system that the old response is no longer required.

✦ Replace with ritual: Choose a new micro-habit that contradicts the inherited behaviour. If you tend to apologise unnecessarily, try replacing it with a heartfelt "Thank you." If you isolate, send a small check-in message to someone who feels safe. If you tend to rush or numb out, allow yourself a two-minute pause—conscious, unhurried, and undeserved by logic but granted by love. These are not resolutions. They are rhythmic acts of remembrance. And rhythm is what rewires you.

"You don't break a loop by force. You break it by rhythm."

Why This Practice Works

Repetitive emotional behaviours are encoded through habit loops—stored in the basal ganglia and reinforced by survival hormones like cortisol and adrenaline. When you introduce a new action alongside somatic calm, the brain begins forming alternative circuits through neuroplasticity. Touch and breath stimulate the vagus nerve, creating safety from within, while reflection engages the insula and prefrontal cortex, inviting conscious choice. What was once reflex can become response—and what was inherited can begin to evolve.

CHAPTER

4

The Mirror Effect – You Become What You're Exposed To

"The environment you tolerate is the identity you slowly absorb."
— Dr. Saif Qazi

"Show me your friends, and I will show you your future." — John Kuebler (paraphrased)

You think your thoughts are entirely your own. Your habits come from discipline. Your choices are products of free will.

But often, what we call 'ourselves' is simply the emotional residue of what we've been repeatedly exposed to.

The people you spend time with, the tone of your childhood home, the language of your culture, the emotional states you normalize — these don't just influence your behaviour. They shape your biology.

You absorb the anxiety of a household that lived in survival mode. You inherit the emotional tightness of elders who suppressed their grief. You mirror the silence of classrooms where curiosity was punished.

And the more you're exposed to something, the more your nervous system memorizes it — even if it was never meant for you.

This isn't imitation. It's biology.

The Biology of Absorption

In the 1990s, Italian neuroscientists discovered **mirror neurons** — brain cells that fire not just when you perform an action, but when you observe someone else doing it.

This explains why you wince when someone stubs their toe. Why a tense room makes you feel breathless. Why a calm presence can settle your heart without a word.

Your brain is wired to reflect. Your body is wired to receive. Your nervous system doesn't ask for permission. It adapts.

A 2019 Harvard study confirmed: just **two minutes** of exposure to someone else's stress can activate your **limbic system** — the emotional command centre of the brain.

You don't have to agree with someone to absorb their emotional state. You simply need to be around them.

"Environment isn't just influence. It's installation."

- Sit next to someone anxious, and your breath may shallow.
- Watch someone live in scarcity, and your body may fear stillness.
- Spend time with emotionally avoidant people, and your nervous system may confuse vulnerability with threat.

  "You are the average of the five people you spend the most time with." — Jim Rohn *(widely quoted, emotionally resonant)*

  This isn't weakness. It's attunement. But if left unconscious, it becomes entrapment.

Echo Story: Meera and the Hustle Spell

Meera wasn't lazy. She was exhausted.

In her twenties, she called herself ambitious. Worked through lunch. Replied to emails past midnight. Felt guilty for resting.

But her body called it something else: survival.

It started when she was ten. Her father lost his job. Her mother rationed food. Her father paced through nights. The house never said "hustle," but Meera's mirror neurons learned:

"If I stop, we fall."

Even after she became financially stable, her body couldn't unlearn the vigilance.

She wasn't chasing success. She was mirroring instability. Her nervous system still thought safety came only from motion.

Her healing didn't begin with rest. It began with realising that stillness wasn't laziness—it was reclamation.

Cultural Reflection: Echoes from Indian Upbringing

Many of us grew up in emotional ecosystems that echoed warnings:

- "Don't fly too high."
- "What will people say?"
- "Success comes through pain."
- "You're lucky we even allow this much."

These weren't just words. They were emotional codes—passed through tone, glances, gestures. Not always cruel. But always clear.

Repeated often enough, they taught your nervous system:

- Dream small to stay safe.
- Appear strong, even when you're struggling.
- Trust exhaustion over ease.

This is how cultural conditioning becomes cellular. Not because you believe it—but because you rehearsed it with your entire being.

"You didn't inherit fear in your thoughts. You memorized it in your breath."

The Influence Audit

Take a soft inventory of your emotional exposure:

Inner Circle — Who do you speak to daily? Do they shrink you or steady you?
Middle Circle — What media, voices, and beliefs do you consume? What moods do they amplify?
Outer Circle — What norms govern your larger world? What is silently praised or punished?

Ask:

- Who around me feels like a nervous system I'd want to borrow?
- What emotional tone do I absorb without noticing?
- Which patterns belong to someone else, but now wear my name?

You're not just what you think. You're what your nervous system rehearses. And what it rehearses depends on what it's around.

And you don't have to cut everything away. You just need to curate.

Final Whisper

If you feel unlike yourself lately, ask: *Who have I been mirroring?*

You might be reflecting someone else's fear. Someone else's urgency. Someone else's silence.

But mirrors aren't destiny. They're design.

You don't need to change your essence. You just need to soften the exposure.

Sacred Reflection

What emotional weather have you mistaken as your own? And what would it take to step into a different climate—one that reflects who you really are?

- Which patterns belong to someone else, but now wear my name?

  You're not just what you think. You're what your nervous system rehearses. And what it rehearses depends on what it's around.

  And you don't have to cut everything away. You just need to

✿ Bonus Practice: Science Soothing

Curate Your Mirror – Emotional Hygiene as a Daily Ritual

You become what you're around—not because you lack identity, but because your nervous system reflects its environment before it questions it. Every day, your emotional state is quietly sculpted by exposure, repetition, and proximity. The work begins not with control, but with curation.

✦ Identify one consistent source of emotional depletion in your life. It might be a social media feed that unsettles you, a conversation that leaves you hollow, or a place that drains your presence. Without anger or avoidance, simply reduce your exposure to it for the next seven days—not as punishment, but as a boundary made of clarity.

✦ Invite one steady source of emotional regulation into your daily rhythm. It could be five minutes of instrumental music that soothes you, a walk without your phone, the voice of a trusted friend, or even a spiritual reminder that helps you return to your centre. Increase your time with this source gently, as if offering your nervous system a daily sip of calm.

✦ Reflect each night—not with judgment, but with curiosity. Ask yourself: What emotional state did I absorb today? Did it reflect the version of life I want to feel more of? What can I choose to un-mirror tomorrow? These questions are not meant to distance you from life. They are meant to return you to it, with choice rather than compulsion.

This isn't about building walls. It's about building awareness.

"What you expose yourself to **repeatedly** doesn't just shape your mood. It trains your biology to belong there."

Why This Practice Works

Your brain is wired with mirror neurons—specialised cells that fire both when you act and when you observe others acting. This biological empathy helps you learn, connect, and adapt, but it also makes you vulnerable to emotional contagion. Over time, repeated exposure to stress or scarcity-based environments activates the limbic system, keeping you in a subtle state of alert. When you deliberately increase exposure to regulated, safe emotional cues, you begin to recondition your nervous system through a process called social co-regulation. What you absorb is what you become—but with awareness, you can choose the emotional mirrors that serve your wholeness.

CHAPTER

5

Hidden Agreements – When Relationships Echo Old Survival Scripts

"Sometimes the cost of love is silence. And sometimes silence becomes your language — even when no one is asking for it anymore." — Dr. Saif Qazi

"You don't fear intimacy. You fear the exposure that once cost you safety."
— Dr. Saif Qazi

You don't remember agreeing to this.
But your body nods yes when your mouth wants to say no.
Your smile stretches even when your heart clenches.
You hold back your truth — not because you're dishonest, but because your nervous system has memorised the shape of being safe.

Somewhere in your story, you learned: *love requires less of me.*
And so, without knowing it, you entered an agreement — not written, not spoken, but lived.
A silent contract with connection that says:

- "If I stay quiet, you'll stay close."
- "If I don't take up space, you won't walk away."
- "If I give more than I have, I'll finally be enough."

These are your hidden agreements — unconscious survival scripts born in childhood, replayed in adult relationships.
They aren't signs of weakness. They're signs of adaptation.
And adaptation, by nature, is intelligent.

You didn't choose this from a place of logic.
You chose it from a place of longing.
Longing to belong.
Longing to be safe.
Longing to be loved without consequence.

Where These Agreements Begin

Children are relational beings. We don't survive through reason. We survive through resonance.

If love was loud but unpredictable…

If warmth arrived but always left too soon…

If anger meant abandonment…

You learned quickly to ask a silent question:

What must I become so I don't get left behind?

In nervous system language, this is called **fawning** — a stress response that doesn't look like panic or fight. It looks like pleasing. Appeasing. Performing. It looks like smiling through discomfort. Saying "yes" before you've checked with yourself. Shrinking not because you want to — but because that's where safety used to live.

"You didn't choose people-pleasing. You chose protection."

"When we are not allowed to feel, we learn to perform." — Bessel van der Kolk

And you chose well — for who you were, and what you knew back then.

The Neuroscience of Over-Accommodation

The part of your nervous system that supports safe connection — the **ventral vagal complex** — needs consistent relational safety to grow strong. But when that safety is missing, your body finds another route: bonding through anxiety.

In a study from the University of Wisconsin, researchers found that individuals with early relational trauma had **increased oxytocin release** during high-stress interactions. Not joy — but bonding under pressure. Their biology tried harder to attach when they felt they might be rejected.

What looks like overgiving may actually be a **neurochemical survival strategy**.
A body negotiating for belonging through over-functioning.

"You're not too much. You're just too alone with the weight you carry." — Hafiz

When you start recognising this, something beautiful happens:
You stop blaming yourself for the patterns you created in the dark.
And you start offering yourself the safety you once begged others for.

Echo Story: Anika and the Pact of Perfection

Anika had been the peacemaker her whole life.
In her family, love was rationed. Affection was conditional.
Approval was earned by achievement.

So she learned to anticipate everyone's needs before they spoke.
To detect disappointment in raised eyebrows.
To apologise for things no one even noticed.

Even in her marriage, she continued the contract:

- "If I'm perfect, he won't leave."
- "If I don't complain, this will stay okay."

But inside, she felt hollow.
Like a beautiful house with no furniture.

In therapy, her counsellor didn't ask her to be louder.
They asked her to *notice.*

To notice how her breath shortened when someone frowned.

To notice how her back tensed when she said, "I'm fine."
To notice how kindness always came with cost.

That's when she realised:
She'd never been dishonest.
She'd just been **loyal** — to a rule that once kept her safe.

"Her silence wasn't a flaw. It was a pact."

Cultural Reflection: Obedience as Love

In many Indian homes, love was equated with compliance:

- "Good children don't talk back."
- "Adjusting is maturity."
- "Be the bigger person."

So emotional discomfort was translated into duty.
Anger became disrespect.
Sadness became weakness.
Silence became strength.
And slowly, generations signed the same contract:

- Give up your truth, gain acceptance.
- Tolerate more, be loved more.
- Shrink gently, and you will belong.

These teachings were not malicious.
They were ancestral scripts — shaped by survival, passed down without question.
But what was sacred for one generation may become suffocating for the next.

Healing doesn't dishonour your parents.
It honours the parts of them that never felt safe enough to do what you now dare to do.

"You are allowed to renegotiate the terms of your emotional contracts."

Final Whisper

Your nervous system isn't betraying you. It's keeping old promises.
But you've grown now. You can offer yourself the safety you once bargained for.
This is not selfish. It's sacred.

Breaking the contract doesn't mean you don't care.
It means you finally care enough to stay whole.

Sacred Reflection

What quiet agreement have you lived by in your closest relationships? And what new sentence would feel more true, more freeing, more yours?

✱ Bonus Practice: Science Soothing

Rewriting the Agreement

Not all healing begins with doing more. Sometimes it begins with doing less of what keeps you hidden.

✱ Choose one emotional contract your body still obeys. It might sound like: "I must be calm to be loved," or "If I express need, I will be rejected." Name it clearly, without judgment.

✱ Place your hand on your chest. Feel the shape of that old agreement sitting quietly in your body. Breathe into that space, slowly and steadily, as if introducing a new rhythm.

✱ Whisper aloud: "I no longer need to disappear to stay close."

✱ Now, take one small act that breaks the contract gently. Let a message wait without guilt. Say "I need a minute" without apology. Let someone feel disappointed without rushing in to fix it. Not to hurt them. But to honour the part of you that no longer wants to be hurt by hiding.

"You don't need to fight for space. You just need to stop abandoning your own."

Why This Practice Works

Chronic people-pleasing activates the sympathetic nervous system — keeping your body on alert to maintain external approval. When you pause and speak a boundary aloud, you engage the **prefrontal cortex**, interrupting the automatic fear response. Placing your hand over your chest stimulates the **vagus nerve**, sending signals of calm and safety. Over time, this conscious interruption — followed by a small self-affirming act — reconditions your nervous system to associate boundaries with safety, not danger.

PART TWO

The Silent Architects of Your Survival

CHAPTER

6

The Inherited Freeze – When Your Body Says No Without Words

"You weren't indecisive. You were in protection mode. Stillness is what your body learned when choice felt unsafe." — Dr. Saif Qazi

You're staring at your phone. You've read the message. You even know what you want to say. But your fingers don't move. Your throat tightens. Your body folds in on itself — like a pause that became permanent.

And then comes the judgment: *Why am I like this?*

But what if this stillness wasn't failure? What if it was ancestral muscle memory? What if freeze is not absence — but adaptation?

You weren't born still. You rehearsed stillness. You inherited it.

What Is Freeze, Really?

Most people know about fight or flight. But the third survival response — **freeze** — is quieter, harder to name. It's the moment your body becomes a question mark. It's the word that gets lost in your throat. It's the conversation you rehearse but never have.

Freeze isn't a choice. It's a learned protection.

If your childhood taught you that speaking up led to chaos…
If your silence earned you safety…
If invisibility became the price for peace…

Then your body chose stillness to survive.

"Freeze isn't weakness. It's unspoken intelligence."

"The body says what words cannot." — Martha Graham

The Nervous System Behind the Stillness

Freeze lives in your **dorsal vagal nerve**, part of the parasympathetic nervous system. When activated, it pulls your physiology into conservation mode: heart rate slows, digestion halts, muscles collapse inward. You appear calm — but inside, you're shut down.

This is why freeze feels like fog.

Like watching yourself through glass.

Like you left your voice behind in another room.

Studies from the National Institute of Mental Health show that people with a history of emotional neglect or unpredictable care are more likely to default to freeze in adulthood — even in non-threatening situations.

"You're not procrastinating. You're preserving. You're not avoiding. You're obeying old nervous system codes."

Echo Story: Taran and the Vanishing Voice

Taran was always the calm one. Polite. Professional. Unshakable. But inside, he was suffocating on the words he never said.

In meetings, he'd freeze. In relationships, he'd vanish. Every time conflict arose, it felt like his mind unplugged. Like the words were somewhere behind him, unreachable.

When he began therapy, he didn't have a trauma story — just a childhood where anger was dangerous, where noise ended in slammed doors and shattered plates. Where fear arrived in the form of *"Keep your mouth shut if you know what's good for you."*

His therapist asked him to hum. Not speak. Just hum. A lullaby his grandmother used to sing. And as he hummed, something moved. A tightness unwound. His body, after years of stillness, began to believe movement was safe again.

Healing didn't come from shouting. It came from sound.

Cultural Reflection: Stillness As Safety

In many Indian families, silence is sainted. Obedience is praised. Quietness is mistaken for maturity. So, children become experts at shrinking. Boys taught not to cry. Girls trained to fold into shadows. All rewarded for stillness. But underneath, the freeze takes root.

In Tamil homes, they say "summa iru" — just stay quiet. In Malayalam: "sheelam vechu irikkuka" — sit with good behaviour. But beneath every well-mannered child may lie a body aching to thaw.

"What you called a personality might just be a survival posture."

The Biology of Thawing

To thaw is not to force. It's to coax.

The **ventral vagus**, the branch responsible for safety and connection, is activated by gentle engagement: breath, humming, soft touch, warmth.

One study showed that 6–8 weeks of daily somatic cues — even as simple as humming or finger tapping — could reduce functional freeze symptoms in adults with complex childhood histories.

This is not instant. It's irrigation.

The nervous system doesn't unlearn in breakthroughs. It softens in repetition.

"Healing isn't loud. It's the quiet permission to move again."

Final Whisper

You were not born frozen. You froze to survive.

And now? The freeze has served you. It bought you time. It bought you safety. It bought you belonging.

But it doesn't need to be your rhythm anymore.

You can speak. You can stir. You can arrive.

"Stillness once saved you. Movement can return you."

Sacred Reflection

What have you mistaken as calm — that might actually be freeze? And what one soft movement would remind your body it's allowed to re-enter?

✱ Bonus Practice: Science Soothing

Thawing the Freeze

Begin slowly. Let your body guide the pace — not your mind. Freeze isn't something you break through. It's something you dissolve, like warmth meeting frost.

✱ First, notice where freeze lives in your body. Does your throat tighten? Does your chest feel caved in? Is your jaw clenched or numb? These are not flaws — they are freeze signatures waiting to thaw.

✱ Place your hand gently over that part. Inhale for a count of four, exhale for six. As you breathe, hum softly — even just a single note. Let the vibration become a signal of safety, reintroducing movement where stillness once settled.

✱ Now move one small part of your body. Wiggle a toe. Tap your fingers slowly. Press your ring finger to your lips and whisper, "It's safe to speak." Let that whisper reach your nervous system, not just your ears.

✱ Finally, close your eyes and imagine a spoon of warm ghee melting through that tightness. Let it spread — through your chest, your back, your voice. This image is not childish. It's somatic. And your body understands it better than logic.

This isn't about doing. It's about softening. Not about forcing movement — but remembering that movement is allowed.

Why This Practice Works

The freeze response is governed by the **dorsal vagal branch** of the parasympathetic nervous system — it slows your body to protect you when escape doesn't feel possible. While it helps in danger, chronic freeze can leave you feeling stuck, numb, or invisible even in safe situations.

Gentle actions like **humming**, **slow breath**, and **micro-movements** send signals to the brainstem that the threat has passed. These cues activate the **ventral vagus nerve**, which supports social engagement and calm.

When you pair soft movement with internal imagery (like warm ghee spreading), it engages the **insula** — the part of your brain that processes internal sensations — helping your body trust sensation again. This is not just mental work. It's body work. And repeated gently, it helps your system return from shutdown to safety — without force, without fear.

CHAPTER

7

The Body That Remembers – When Your Past Lives in Your Present

"The body speaks in fossils—every tension a preserved memory."
— Dr. Saif Qazi

The Confusing War Within

You set a goal. You feel inspired. You make progress. And then—something inside you slows down. You delay. You downplay. You distract. Not because you're lazy. Not because you don't care. But because your body remembers a time when visibility came at a cost. A time when standing out led to rejection. When wanting more led to punishment.

Western books may call this sabotage or fear of success. But this isn't pathology. It's intelligence. This is the body that remembers.

What Is the Body That Remembers?

The body that remembers is the part of you still loyal to old survival codes. It says:

"Don't shine—they'll mock you."

"Don't rest—you'll fall behind."

"Don't be too much—you'll be left."

It doesn't care about growth. It cares about safety. If joy once led to heartbreak, or success once led to exile, your body will equate expansion with danger. It whispers: "Stay small. Stay safe."

"The body keeps the score: it remembers what the mind forgets." — Bessel van der Kolk

In Ayurveda, this is sanchita—the accumulated impressions we carry. In neuroscience, it's implicit memory. You need neither label to feel its weight.

Why the Brain Fears Growth

Your basal ganglia—the habit centre of your brain—can't tell time. A 20-year-old shame lives in your nerves like it's now. When Dinesh's boss praised him, his throat tightened. Later, he remembered being eight, reciting a poem at a wedding, and hearing his uncle sneer: "Who does he think he is?" His body had remembered before his mind did. Modern science calls this "negativity bias." Your ancestors called it "staying alive."

Echo Story: Dinesh and the Promotion He Didn't Want

Dinesh had always been the quiet achiever. Dependable. Brilliant. Humble. When he was offered a major promotion—the role he had always wanted—he smiled outwardly. But inside, panic stirred. He delayed. Missed paperwork. Skipped a key meeting. He told himself he was being practical. But his body was reliving something it had never resolved.

A memory surfaced: age 14, school debate. He had shone. Friends mocked him. One stopped speaking to him. That night, he lay awake tracing the crack in his bedroom wall where his father had once thrown a glass. His body learned: brilliance precedes rupture. The next morning, his mother oiled his hair in silence. The unspoken lesson: *Better to blend in than burn.*

That day, his nervous system wrote a rule: *Visibility costs belonging.* Decades later, his body was still enforcing it. He wasn't afraid of failure. He was afraid of exile.

The Root Conflict: Safety vs. Expansion

Most self-help advice says "push through." But your body doesn't respond to force. It responds to familiarity. Growth feels threatening not because it's wrong—but because it's unknown. New versions of you often require saying more, needing more, being more. If those acts were once punished, your body will resist not from weakness, but from wisdom.

This is not a ritual. It's recognition.

Cultural Reflection: Belonging and Betrayal

In Igbo culture, there's a proverb: "The moon moves slowly, but it crosses the town." Contrast this with the Hindi saying: *Tez chalo, par chupke se* (Walk fast, but quietly).

In Marwari business homes, success is celebrated—but only within caste lines. In Bengali circles, brilliance is welcome—if it stays modest. In Tamil Brahmin homes, ambition is respected—but discipline is revered.

Your body learns its pace from these whispers. It is not rejecting joy. It is protecting connection.

Final Whisper

Your body isn't a traitor—it's the last loyalist to a fading regime. Today, you are both the revolution and the amnesty.

Sacred Reflection

Where does your body still kneel at old altars? And where is it already stretching toward sun?

✱ Bonus Practice: Science Soothing

The Permission Experiment

When you feel stuck, don't force your way out. Pause. Let the moment breathe.

✱ Ask softly: "What old rule is my body still obeying?" Perhaps it's "Don't speak up," or "Stay small to stay safe." These were once protections — not problems.

* Place a hand over your chest. Whisper: "Thank you for keeping me safe. We can try a new way now." Let your body feel that shift, even if it's subtle.

* Notice your breath. Your posture. What softens? That softening is not small. It's your nervous system learning that safety doesn't have to mean silence.

Why This Practice Works

Feeling stuck is often a signal from your **amygdala**, which flags anything unfamiliar as unsafe — even growth. By pausing and naming the "rule" behind the freeze, you engage the **prefrontal cortex**, allowing reflection instead of reflex.

The phrase "Thank you for keeping me safe" helps calm the **hypothalamic-pituitary-adrenal (HPA) axis**, reducing stress signals and building trust between old patterns and new intentions. This softens internal resistance without triggering fear.

When you observe your breath or posture shift, you're strengthening **interoceptive awareness** — a function of the **insula** — which helps your body recognise safety. Over time, this repetition rewires your default response through **neuroplasticity**.

CHAPTER

8

The Quiet Exhaustion – When You're Doing Everything Right and Still Feel Hollow

"You have the resume of someone who's winning at life—and the nervous system of someone who's still bracing for war."
— Dr. Saif Qazi
"There is no greater burden than carrying a self you no longer recognize."
— Imam Al-Ghazali (Adapted)

The Performance That Never Ends

This isn't laziness. This isn't ingratitude. This is unprocessed survival running your nervous system on a loop. You're not chasing success anymore. You're chasing the safety success once promised.

In our culture, we rarely say "I'm overwhelmed." We say "I'm managing." We carry exhaustion like a medal and call it strength. But silence doesn't heal. Awareness does.

The Science of Overdrive

Your brain's wiring isn't designed purely for ambition—it's designed for survival. When safety is linked to achievement early in life—through family praise, societal rewards, or survival needs—your nervous system learns a dangerous shortcut:

Effort = Safety.
Rest = Risk.

"Rest is not idleness, and to lie sometimes on the grass... is by no means a waste of time." — John Lubbock

A 2017 study at Stanford University showed that children raised under high emotional pressure often develop hypervigilant brains—constantly scanning for errors, even in peaceful conditions. Later in life, these same brains confuse calm with danger and overwork to feel safe. You're not just working hard. You're biologically negotiating for permission to exist.

Echo Story 1: Irfan and the Unfinished Ladder

Irfan grew up in Hyderabad, in a modest household where every rupee mattered. His father often reminded him, "If you don't climb high, you'll be crushed." Irfan climbed. Top of his class. Early promotions. A house before thirty.

And yet every night, he lay awake calculating new goals—as if joy was hidden in the next checkbox. One evening, after receiving an award, Irfan sat alone in his car, feeling a heavy emptiness. He had climbed every ladder handed to him. But the ladder had no top. Because it wasn't built for fulfilment. It was built for survival. And no achievement could undo the nervous system that still braced for collapse.

Familiar Pain Over Unknown Joy

Why do smart, self-aware people sabotage their own rest? Because the brain prefers familiar pain over unfamiliar peace. MRI scans show that when presented with unfamiliar positive experiences (like praise, rest, or abundance), the limbic system—the brain's emotional centre—often lights up in fear, not joy.
Joy feels like a risk if your nervous system was trained in survival.

This is why:
Rest feels uncomfortable.
Praise feels suspicious.
Stability feels temporary.

You are not lazy. You are not ungrateful. You are biologically cautious.

Echo Story 2: Sneha and the Ghost of Exhaustion

Sneha grew up in a coastal town in Kerala, where her mother ran a small grocery shop alone after her father's sudden passing. Sneha learned early:

Rest is selfish.
Work is redemption.
Survival is an everyday exam.

As a child, the smell of her mother's shop clung to her: turmeric and dust, ambition and exhaustion.

As an adult, even after financial stability arrived, Sneha couldn't sit still. Vacations made her anxious. Success tasted like unfinished homework. One day, after a near collapse at her desk, Sneha's therapist asked her a simple question:

"Whose exhaustion are you still carrying?"

Sneha realized—she was living not her dreams, but her mother's unfinished survival script.

Echo Story 3: Amarjeet and the Inherited Guilt

Amarjeet, a young engineer from Punjab, was the pride of his village. Scholarships, achievements, job offers—he earned them all. But no matter how much he achieved, a quiet guilt followed him:

A guilt for enjoying rest.
A guilt for buying comfort.

A guilt for smiling when his family still remembered struggle.

In his heart, Amarjeet had internalized a dangerous rule: **"If my ancestors suffered, I must honour them by suffering too."**

He wasn't ungrateful. He was grieving a childhood where joy felt like betrayal. Amarjeet wasn't chasing dreams. He was repaying invisible debts.

The Under Mourner Within

You are not tired because you're weak. You're tired because you've been attending a funeral no one announced—the funeral of the self you had to bury to survive.

Without grief, victories feel hollow. Without mourning, the nervous system stays stuck in "what's next?"

You don't need more achievement. You need permission to feel safe without it. You don't just need to dream bigger. You need to forgive yourself for surviving.

The Indian Over Functioning Spell

In Bengali folklore, there's a tale of a koel bird kept in a golden cage. Every morning it sang for its captors, and every evening, it dreamed of forests it had never seen. One day, the door was left open. But the koel didn't leave. It had memorised the price of flying too young.

You hear it everywhere:
In Indian families, ambition is often a duty. The oldest child? Expected to uplift everyone. The brightest one?

Expected to set the standard. The emotionally strongest? Expected to carry unspoken grief.

You hear it everywhere:
"Don't forget where you came from."
"Make us proud."
"Your success is our only hope."

In our culture, love often comes with an unspoken ledger: *"We sacrificed, so you must overachieve."* But healing begins when you realize—you don't owe your ancestors your joy. You honour them by living what they couldn't.

These are not cruel expectations. They are survival echoes. But surviving is not the same as living. You are allowed to outgrow the spell without breaking your belonging.

Final Whisper

You were never meant to earn your right to rest. You were born worthy of it. The marathon is over. The finish line was a mirage. Put down the baton. Breathe.

Sacred Reflection

Where does your body still chase enoughness—and what might it feel like to simply arrive?

✱ Bonus Practice: Science Soothing

Safety Beyond Success

Each night, name three ways you are already safe—without performing.
A roof. A kind voice. A quiet breath. Let your body hear: *"I am not in danger just because I paused."*

Practice one act of gentle rest daily. Five minutes of silence. A slow meal. A small no. Let rest feel safe—not earned.

Then place your hand on your chest and whisper: *"I no longer owe survival for my right to exist."*

Finally, offer your body a moment of joy without purpose. Sing, doodle, dance off-camera, or call someone just to laugh. Let joy arrive without permission slips.

"Your nervous system doesn't just need rest. It needs rest without guilt."

Why This Practice Works

Success-based survival often trains the nervous system to equate rest with danger. This practice helps reverse that. Naming current safety activates the **prefrontal cortex**, reorienting attention away from imagined threat. Repetitive rest and joy cues retrain the **amygdala** to associate pause with safety, not punishment.

Placing a hand over the chest engages the **vagus nerve**, which downshifts the **sympathetic nervous system** and promotes emotional regulation. Joy without outcome lights up the **dopaminergic reward system**, helping your body relearn that pleasure doesn't require performance. Over time, this rewires internal metrics of safety from achievement to presence.

CHAPTER

9

The Fear of Joy – Why Happiness Sometimes Feels Dangerous

"The body flinches at joy not because it's unworthy of it, but because it remembers the aftermath."
— Dr. Saif Qazi
"There is no greater sorrow than to recall a time of joy in misery."
— Dante Alighieri

When Joy Feels Like a Setup

You prepare for sorrow like monsoons—expected, seasonal. But joy? Joy arrives like sudden sunshine in

December. You squint. You shield. You wait for the clouds to return.

Because joy feels unfamiliar. Unsafe. Suspicious.

It arrives like sunlight through a window you forgot existed—and your body pulls the curtain. Not because it doesn't want the light, but because it remembers the last time it danced in it—and got burned.

You've felt this:
A compliment that made you uneasy.
A good day that made you anxious.
A moment of laughter that made you brace.

This isn't because you're ungrateful.
It's because your nervous system hasn't learned that joy is safe.

"Joy is the most vulnerable emotion we experience." — Brené Brown

Joy becomes a warning signal. A prelude to the fall.

Echo Story: Neeraj and the Birthday That Hurt

Neeraj grew up in Mumbai, in a home where joy had consequences.

When he laughed too loudly, his father snapped: "Stop being silly." When he brought home good grades, his relatives said, "Don't show off." When he celebrated anything, someone would mention someone else who was suffering more.

On his 10th birthday, his mother decorated the house. Friends came. Cake was cut. He hid behind the sheer curtain as guests arrived, the fabric cool and scratchy against his cheek. Later that night, a relative remarked, "All this tamasha for one child? Don't forget the world is suffering." The smell of vanilla icing still lingered.

That night, Neeraj cried silently. Not because he was scolded—but because he was ashamed of his own happiness.

Now 34, Neeraj lives abroad. He earns well. He is loved. But on his birthday, he always feels a strange tightness in his chest. He skips parties. Turns off his phone.

He says, "I'm just not into birthdays."

But the truth is: joy still feels like something to apologise for.

Last year, his partner surprised him with a cake. His hands froze around the knife, the weight of the blade suddenly foreign. He blew the candles—then immediately shared slices with neighbours, diluting the celebration like chai made 'for everyone' in his childhood home.

Cultural Reflection: *Nazar* and the Suspicion Around Joy

In many Indian homes, joy doesn't come unaccompanied. It is shadowed by precaution. Every celebration is tempered with warnings:

- "Don't say too much."
- "Nazar lag jayegi." *(Someone will cast an evil eye.)*
- "Celebrate quietly."

Across cultures—Latin America's *mal de ojo*, Arab culture's *evil eye*, African warnings to "not outshine," East Asia's reverence for restraint—there is a shared belief: joy made visible invites harm. We begin to treat happiness like a diya in the wind—too bright, too exposed, too easy to extinguish.

So we shield it. Dim it. Distrust it.

But when did we forget that light, by nature, demands to be seen?

We treat recovery like a wedding—something to be seen, photographed, celebrated on schedule. But grief and grace are monsoon rains: they arrive when they will, and the earth knows better than to demand an explanation.

We internalise this vigilance until it becomes reflex. You smile and scan. You succeed and shrink. You laugh and flinch. Joy becomes something to manage—not something to inhabit.

As psychiatrist Dr. Bessel van der Kolk writes in *The Body Keeps the Score*, "The body responds to intense emotions—even positive ones—based on memory, not logic." Which means joy can feel like danger if the last time you felt it, it was followed by a slap, a silence, or a loss.

To reclaim joy, we must first uncouple it from dread. Not spiritually. Biologically. And slowly. Because while suffering becomes familiar, joy must be remembered anew.

Science Insight: Why the Brain Distrusts Joy

Joy, from a neurobiological perspective, is not a simple light switch. It is a full-body risk assessment. Especially for trauma survivors, joy can activate not only the brain's reward systems but also its threat detection networks. The amygdala, long associated with fear and vigilance, often lights up even in response to positive stimuli when the nervous system has a history of unpredictability or emotional loss.

This happens because the brain doesn't register emotions as "good" or "bad"—only as *familiar* or *unfamiliar*, *safe* or *potentially dangerous.*

In a 2016 fMRI study published in *Nature Neuroscience*, researchers observed that trauma-impacted brains often respond to joyful imagery with the same physiological vigilance as they do to distress cues. This paradox—of pleasure triggering protection—can make joy feel unsafe. Dr. Richard Davidson's research at the University of Wisconsin deepens this finding: individuals with histories of emotional neglect show increased activity in the insular cortex, the brain's self-surveillance hub.

The result?

The body becomes hyper-attuned, suspicious of ease. For the traumatized brain, joy flickers like a candle in a room where the wind once tore through—the body braces for the gust even when the air is still.

This is why Neeraj's chest tightens on birthdays. It's not mood. It's mechanism. His insular cortex is scanning the environment the way his grandmother once scanned the room after good news, whispering "nazar lag jayegi." *(Someone will cast an evil eye.)*

- You smile, then feel watched.

- You laugh, then feel guilt.
- You succeed, then sabotage.

The body flinches because it doesn't yet trust the good.

Somatic Insight: Where Joy Feels Unsafe

Joy lives in the body as expansion:
Open chest. Soft belly. Relaxed jaw. Dilated pupils.

But if your body once associated expansion with exposure, and exposure with danger, then joy will feel like threat.

You'll smile and then scan the room.
You'll succeed and then wait for something to go wrong.
You'll fall in love—and immediately imagine the ending.

This isn't neurosis. It's survival math.
But it can be rewritten—slowly, safely.

Final Whisper

Your joy is not arrogance.
It is not foolish.
It is not a betrayal of the suffering around you.

It is a return.
It is a soft rebellion against despair.
It is your nervous system remembering that light doesn't always burn.

You don't need to apologise for joy.
You just need to stay with it long enough for your body to believe it.

Joy is not the prelude to the fall. It is the ground returning to your feet.

Sacred Reflection

When was the last time you cut your joy short because it felt "too much"?
Where in your body do you feel the fear of joy most acutely?
What would your joy look like if no one was watching?
What memory would you reclaim if joy stopped feeling like a threat?
And what would it mean to let your nervous system linger in the light, just a little longer next time?

✱ Bonus Practice: Science Soothing

The Rehearsal of Joy

Joy returns through gentle rehearsal — not as a performance, but as a permission.

✱ Recall a memory where you felt safe and joyful, even briefly. Let it play in your mind like a quiet film. Feel how your body responds.

✱ Inhale: "It's okay to feel good."
Exhale: "I don't need to shrink to stay safe."

✱ Give your body one small joy daily — sunlight, music, laughter, or silence. Speak your joy aloud, even softly: "This is mine. It's allowed."

✱ Let your smile meet your own eyes in the mirror. Whisper: "This light belongs to you."

✱ Light a candle and let its glow soften you. Whisper: *"This joy is borrowed from the Divine."*

Why This Practice Works

People who've experienced chronic stress often associate joy with vulnerability or danger. Recalling joyful memories activates the **hippocampus**, which helps rewire emotional associations in the brain. Soft breath and affirmations engage the **ventral vagus nerve**, shifting the body from defence to openness.

Daily micro-joys act like safe emotional exposures, teaching the nervous system that pleasure can arrive without punishment. Over time, joy stops feeling risky and starts feeling real.

CHAPTER

10

The Emotional Cost of Safety – When Protection Becomes a Prison

"Safety isn't always sanctuary. Sometimes it's just the most beautiful cage you learned to decorate."
— Dr. Saif Qazi
"If you avoid danger in the long run, you cease to live at all."
— C.S. Lewis

The Cage You Called Home

You've built a life that feels steady. Predictable. Safe. Nothing hurts too much. Nothing shakes too hard. You've avoided the chaos, sidestepped the storms, and mapped out your days like well-planned routes on familiar roads. You've built a life where the floors don't shake—but neither do the walls echo with your laughter anymore.

But if you listen closely, there's a silence beneath the safety. A hollowness. A stillness that doesn't soothe—but suffocates.

Because sometimes, the cost of protection is permission. The cost of control is connection. And the cost of never being unsafe… is never being fully alive.

When Safety Becomes a Spell

Your nervous system is hardwired for survival, not satisfaction. In childhood, if chaos followed expression, your brain learned to associate quietness with safety. If joy was interrupted by loss, your body learned to prepare for absence even in presence.

So you build rituals to feel safe: saying yes when you mean no. Avoiding risk even when the soul aches for expansion. Holding back tears, laughter, anger—until your own aliveness begins to rust inside you.

A 2020 paper from the Journal of Neuroscience found that individuals with high threat sensitivity often suppress emotional responses not consciously—but automatically. A threat-sensitive brain often mistakes suppression for safety—like Nila's hands automatically steadying the cup before it could rattle the table. What feels like choice is often an old agreement: stay small, stay safe, stay silent.

But protection, when repeated too long, becomes a cage. And the body forgets how to stretch its wings.

"Ships are safest in harbour—but that's not what ships are built for." — William Shedd

Echo Story: Nila and the Art of Staying Small

Nila, a 36-year-old ceramic artist from Pune, was known for her softness. She was the peacekeeper in every room, the one who never raised her voice, the one who always anticipated everyone's needs.

She had grown up in a household where her father's temper ruled the walls. A slammed door could silence dinner. A raised voice meant retreat. She learned to be invisible.

To stay safe.

In her adult life, Nila avoided conflict with surgical precision. She never asked for more money from clients. She laughed off late payments. She downplayed her own exhibitions. And when her long-term partner forgot her birthday for the third year in a row, she smiled and said, "It's okay, I don't need much."

But later that night, she stood in the kitchen, holding a cup she had made with her own hands—and it slipped. As it shattered, she realised something: she had curated a life so safe that it no longer had room for her truth. For the first time, she didn't rush to clean up. She watched the fragments—how they caught the light. How they made sound.

Her nervous system had mastered the art of staying small. But her soul was suffocating.

Cultural Reflection: The Virtue of Shrinking

In many Indian families, especially for women, emotional safety is synonymous with invisibility. You're praised for being "adjusting," "low-maintenance," "understanding."

You're taught that compliance is virtue. That saying "I'm fine" is nobler than saying "I'm hurt." That if you can avoid shaking the boat, you'll be rewarded with peace.

But what happens when the peace you're offered comes at the cost of your voice?

In Tamil, there's a saying: *"Idhuve podhum-nu sollradhu, vazhkai illama irukaradhu."*
("Saying 'this is enough' is often how a life disappears.")

We inherit silence like gold jewellery—precious, heavy, leaving marks even after removal.

Safety, in such homes, is not just protection. It's performance. And somewhere along the line, the body forgets it's allowed to be loud. To ask. To ache. To be.

Somatic Insight: The Muscles That Forget

Protection lives in the body. In the hunched shoulders. The shallow breath. The tightened jaw. The rehearsed smile.

When safety has meant self-suppression, the body begins to mute itself automatically. You avoid confrontation not because you're weak, but because your muscles remember that speaking once led to rupture.

This isn't cowardice. It's code. But code can be rewritten. This isn't a flaw. It's an ancient receipt—proof you once paid for joy with pain, and your body never forgot the exchange rate.

Final Whisper

You didn't build this prison.
You inherited it.
Brick by brick from silence.
Bar by bar from love that demanded you shrink to stay safe.

But the door has always been unlocked.

You can leave gently.
You can expand slowly.
You can take your safety with you—and still walk free.

Sacred Reflection

Where have you mistaken silence for peace, invisibility for humility, safety for love?
And what would it mean to grow loud, tender, and whole in the life you were once taught to survive?

✱ Bonus Practice: Science Soothing

Micro-Expansions

Healing isn't always about protection. Sometimes, it's about practicing expansion — one breath, one word, one posture at a time.

✱ Place your hand on your chest and whisper: "It is safe to take up more space than this." Let the body hear it before the mind believes it.

✱ Once a day, speak a small truth — even if it trembles. Don't edit it. Don't make it neat. Just let it rise.
Sufi whisper: "Speak even if your voice shakes — the Beloved leans closer to broken syllables."

✱ Stand. Stretch your arms wide. If you feel resistance, breathe into it. Hold the posture. Let your body remember that expression is not rebellion — it is remembrance.

Why This Practice Works

Suppressed self-expression often creates chronic contraction in the body — shoulders tense, breath shallow, voice hesitant. By combining **gentle vocalisation**, **chest-opening posture**, and **affirming touch**, you stimulate the **vagus nerve** and retrain your nervous system to associate openness with safety. Over time, this reduces social inhibition and fear responses. Small expansions create new neural maps — where truth no longer equals danger, but dignity.

PART THREE

Learning a New Way to Breathe

CHAPTER

11

The Disappearing Act – When You Leave Yourself to Be Loved

"You weren't born to abandon yourself. But somewhere along the way, someone taught you that love requires disappearance."
— Dr. Saif Qazi

"To be fully seen by somebody, then, and be loved anyhow—this is a human offering that can border on miraculous."
— Elizabeth Gilbert

The Cost of Being Chosen

You shape-shifted for love—not with dramatic spells, but with a thousand tiny surrenders: the opinions swallowed, the outfits changed, the dreams downsized before they could be dismissed.

You adjusted, edited, softened. You dimmed your truth, delayed your needs, deleted parts of yourself just to be held. Not because you were weak. But because every memory your body held told you that love is conditional—and safety lies in being who others want, not who you are.

And so, slowly, gently, invisibly—you disappeared.

Not all at once. Not dramatically. But in the quiet, everyday compromises: the movie you didn't say you hated, the job offer you didn't pursue, the laugh you tucked away because it was "too loud," the pain you didn't name because it might rock the boat.

This is not your flaw. This is your conditioning. And it is time to return.

The First Goodbye Was to Yourself

Most people think abandonment is external: someone leaves, someone disappoints, someone betrays. But the deepest form of abandonment isn't when someone else walks away. It's when *you* do.

When you pre-empt rejection by becoming less. When you silence your intuition so someone else can feel safe. When you carry the weight of being liked over the joy of being true.

Neuroscience calls this "fawning"—a survival response where the prefrontal cortex literally hijacks the voice box to appease threat. Arvind's silent hotel room wasn't choice. It was biology remembering old wars.

It's most common in those who grew up with inconsistent affection, volatile caregivers, or emotional enmeshment. In such bodies, the deepest fear is not pain—it's disapproval. Because disapproval once meant emotional exile.

Echo Story: Arvind and the Room That Shrank

Arvind grew up in Delhi in a home where his mother's love was vast but volatile. She adored him—but only when he was polite, well-behaved, grateful. The moment he protested, even gently, her face would shift.

He learned early: love is given to the version of you that causes the least discomfort.

As an adult, Arvind became everyone's favourite. In college, he was the fixer. In his relationships, he anticipated needs before they were spoken. In meetings, he nodded even when his chest burned with disagreement. But inside, a strange hollowness grew. Not sadness. Not anger. Just the quiet ache of someone who hadn't heard his own voice in years.

The moment that changed everything came in a hotel room in Jaipur. His partner had just asked, "Are you happy with me?"

Arvind opened his mouth.

And nothing came out.

Not because there wasn't an answer. But because there were too many versions of him inside—each built to be loved, none built to be true.

He realised: he hadn't lost his voice. He had loaned it out too many times. That night, he stood under the shower until the water ran cold, trying to wash off the performance. His skin remembered what his mind had forgotten: he was still in there somewhere.

Cultural Reflection: The Virtue of Vanishing

In many cultures, especially collectivist ones like India's, the idea of love is often bound to sacrifice. You're praised not for self-expression, but for self-erasure.

- The good daughter doesn't argue.
- The ideal husband provides, not cries.
- The obedient child adjusts, even in unfairness.

We grow up hearing:
"Don't make a scene."
"Think of others."
"Love means compromise."

But what if love becomes a ritual of loss? A rehearsal of quiet exits from ourselves?

In Urdu, there's a phrase: *"Khud ko bhool jaana."*
("To forget oneself.")

It's spoken as praise. But beneath it lives a thousand quiet funerals.

We frame this disappearing as nobility—like lighting a candle from your own wax until only the wick remains.

Somatic Insight: Where You Went Missing

Self-abandonment doesn't live in your mind. It lives in your body.

It's the clench in your throat when you want to say no.
The fake smile at the joke that hurt.
The stomach drops when someone says, "I miss the old you"—and you think maybe you do too.

These are not small acts. They're soul leaks.

But the good news? If you can leave yourself, you can also return.

Final Whisper

You don't need to keep auditioning for love.
You don't need to rehearse someone else's lines.
You don't need to vanish to be seen.

Come back.
To your voice.
To your need.
To your rightful space in the centre of your own life.

You are not too much.
You were just never meant to shrink

Sacred Reflection

What parts of yourself have you been rationing to be accepted?

And what would it feel like to be loved without leaving the room where your soul still waits?

✱ Bonus Practice: Science Soothing

Returning to the Mirror – A Ritual of Reappearance

Disappearance often begins in the mirror — when you stop recognising your own reflection, or begin editing it to match someone else's comfort. This practice invites you to come back to yourself, gently, without performance.

✱ Stand before a mirror. Not to adjust anything. Not to smile for anyone. Just to witness. Let your eyes meet your own — even if it feels strange. Ask softly, "What did I need to hear but never did?" Say the answer aloud, even if it trembles. Even if you don't believe it yet.

✱ Find a childhood photo. Sit with it for a few minutes. Place your hand over your heart and whisper: "You never needed to earn your worth. You were always enough. I see you now. I won't unsee you again."

✱ Each morning for the next 7 days, return to the mirror. Ask: "Who am I becoming when I stop hiding?" Write down what arises. Let the answer be messy. Let it be honest. Let it be yours.

✱ When criticism creeps in — about your face, your body, your path — pause. Press your ring finger to the dip between your collarbones, an Ayurvedic marma point linked to self-trust. Whisper: "My worth is not earned through anyone else's eyes. This time, I'm learning to see — not judge."

This is not vanity. It is reclamation. The mirror is no longer the enemy. It is a witness to your return.

Why This Practice Works

Visual self-recognition, combined with affirming language, activates the **insula** and **medial prefrontal cortex** — regions of the brain responsible for self-awareness and emotional regulation. Adding touch and vocal repetition stimulates the **vagus nerve**, calming the nervous system and rewiring old shame-based narratives. Over time, this practice helps restore a compassionate internal gaze, where your identity is no longer filtered through fear, but grounded in truth.

CHAPTER

12

The Grief, You Didn't Know You Were Carrying – How Loss Hides in the Body, Not Just the Heart

"Some grief doesn't announce itself. It just settles quietly into the tissues, waiting to be named."
— Dr. Saif Qazi

The Quiet Weight You Forgot to Question

Not all grief wears black. Some of it wears your work clothes. Smiles at parties. Pays bills on time. It doesn't sob in corners — it sighs in meetings. It doesn't scream — it stiffens.
Some wears your mother's old sari — folded neatly in memory's cupboard, taken out only when no one is watching.
This is the grief you didn't know you were carrying.

"Sorrow carves the vessel that joy may fill." — Kahlil Gibran

The loss of a version of you that never got to exist. The ache of friendships that slowly faded. The regret of dreams archived quietly because they were "too much." The inherited sorrow passed down like bone structure.

Not all grief is loud. Some of it lives in the body like background noise you forgot to stop noticing.
You function. You achieve. You even laugh. But deep inside, something feels heavier than it should.

The Science of Hidden Grief

Neuroscience shows that the body doesn't differentiate between physical threat and emotional threat. The limbic system responds to loss — whether it's a death, a breakup, or a silent dream slipping away — with the same stress hormones. But when that grief isn't metabolised through mourning, it doesn't vanish. It burrows.

Harvard researchers found that unprocessed grief lingers in the body like an uninvited guest — raising inflammation in joints (those unwept tears) and gut (those unsaid words). You may not have lost a person. But maybe you lost a place, a version of yourself, a future you were building toward.

And the body remembers.

Echo Story: Aanya and the Grief of the Almost

Aanya used to say she had never experienced "real" loss. No funerals in her twenties. No major tragedies. But she was always tired. Her jaw ached. Her chest carried a quiet throb — like missing someone who never existed.

In therapy, it unravelled slowly. Her parents' divorce wasn't loud — it was a quiet fading. Her engagement ended not with drama, but mutual resignation. Her childhood dream of being a dancer was shelved so early she could barely remember it.

No big goodbyes. Just small disappearances. One by one.

She had grieved nothing. But she was grieving everything.

One night, she watched a child dance barefoot at a wedding. And her eyes filled without permission. That was the beginning. She placed her palm on her own chest and whispered:
"I'm sorry I never let you mourn."

That was the funeral her nervous system had been waiting for. The next morning, her shoulders felt lighter — not because the grief had vanished, but because it had finally been witnessed. Even ghosts rest when acknowledged.

Cultural Reflection: When Grief Is Shamed

In many cultures — including ours — there is a silent hierarchy of grief.
You're allowed to mourn death. Maybe divorce. But who gives you permission to mourn the city you left? The language you forgot? The parent you never truly had? The joy you outgrew? The childhood that looked fine but never felt safe?

You're told:
"Be grateful."

"You have it better than most."
"Others have real problems."

So you bury it.

But buried grief doesn't decompose. It grows roots.

In Marathi, there's a proverb:

"मनातलं दुखणं, अंगावर उमटतं."

("Pain held in the mind eventually shows on the body.")

We mourn only what society deems grievable. But the body has its own elegy. And it keeps singing until you listen.

We treat grief like inherited jewellery — locked away except for special occasions, growing heavier with each unworn year.

Somatic Insight: Where Uncried Tears Go

Unfelt grief doesn't disappear. It localises.
It becomes the jaw that clenches at night.
The sigh you let out every time you're alone.
The sleep that doesn't refresh.
The craving for sugar — not to indulge, but to soothe.
The body stores what the heart isn't allowed to speak.
But mourning isn't just crying. It's naming.
It's slowing down. It's letting the body finish the sentence the mind was too proud to start.

These are not weaknesses.
They are unfinished funerals waiting for your presence.

Final Whisper

You don't need to justify your sorrow.
You don't need permission to feel the ache of what never was.
You are allowed to grieve quietly held hopes.

To hold funerals for your "almosts."
To weep for the you that never got to be.

Because the grief you name is the grief that loosens.
And the tears you honour are the ones that free you.

Sacred Reflection

What grief have you carried silently, thinking it wasn't real enough to mourn?
And what might shift if you gave it the funeral it never had — gently, slowly, without shame?

✱ Bonus Practice: Science Soothing

The Silent Funeral – A Ritual for Unspoken Grief

Some grief doesn't need wailing. It needs witnessing.
This is a quiet ritual for the sorrows you never got to name — the ones that didn't earn condolence calls, but still left echoes in your bones.

✱ Begin by sitting with a photo, object, or memory linked to something you've lost — not necessarily a person, but a version of you, a dream, a place, a relationship, even a hope that never fully formed. Let your body remember — not the story, but the sensation.

✱ Place a hand over your chest or the part of your body that clenches when you think of this loss. It could be your throat, your jaw, your belly. Breathe slowly and say softly, "You mattered. Even if no one knew. I remember now."

* Light a candle if you can. Let its flame mark the mourning. This is your funeral. Not for death, but for dignity — for all that quietly exited your life without goodbye.

* Let one tear fall, or one breath deepen. That's enough. This is not about catharsis. It's about completion.

* To close, whisper this blessing: "May what I lost be honoured. May

what I carry be softened. May what still aches know it is allowed to

heal."

This is how grief becomes holy. Not because it is loud. But because it is finally allowed.

Why This Practice Works

Unprocessed grief activates the same **limbic brain circuits** as acute threat. When mourning is suppressed, it creates chronic tension in the **autonomic nervous system** — manifesting as jaw pain, sleep disturbances, digestive issues, and emotional numbing.

Rituals like gentle breath, symbolic witnessing (e.g., candle lighting), and spoken closure engage the **parasympathetic system** via the **vagus nerve**, helping the body feel safe enough to release. Naming the loss allows the **prefrontal cortex** to update the brain's narrative:
"This ended. I survived. I'm allowed to soften now."

This is not a performance. It's biological integration — where grief becomes memory, not muscle.

CHAPTER

13

The Grief of Outgrowing – When Healing Costs Familiar Love

"Sometimes you don't leave people. You just grow where they refuse to water."
— Dr. Saif Qazi
"The price of evolution is that you will lose the comfort of who you were and the approval of those who needed you to stay that way."
— Brianna Wiest

When Growing Feels Like Leaving

No one tells you healing will make you lonely—that expanding into yourself might mean contracting out of old circles, like a tree whose roots now crack the veranda where family once gathered.

That joy, clarity, and self-respect come with a side effect called distance. That the more you learn to honour your truth, the more you begin to outgrow the places that taught you to ignore it.

Sometimes healing feels like betrayal—not because you did anything wrong, but because you stopped doing what kept you approved.

You didn't choose to leave people behind. But you could no longer shrink yourself to stay close.

The Ache of Becoming

There's a quiet ache that comes with choosing yourself.

The childhood friend who no longer calls because you stopped gossiping. The family gathering that feels tighter—not because they changed, but because you did. The parent who says, "You've become too sensitive." The lover who says, "You've changed."

Yes, you have. And that's the grief.

Healing doesn't just feel like light. It feels like rupture.

"A traveler must knock on every door before reaching his own." —
Rumi

It feels like unzipping the identity that once kept you safe and watching it fall to the floor—creased with the expectations of everyone you loved.

Echo Story: Tara and the Unspoken Exit

Tara had always been the emotional glue of her home.

As the eldest daughter in a Punjabi household, she mediated fights, protected her younger siblings, smiled through funerals, hosted everything, and never cried in public. Her mother once said, "You are the strong one in this family." Tara wore it like a crown. And then, like a muzzle.

In her thirties, therapy changed her vocabulary. She began naming feelings. Setting limits. Saying, "That hurt me."

Her family didn't say much. But slowly, the calls reduced. She noticed she wasn't asked to host Diwali anymore. Her brother teased, "Madam is too evolved now.

Tara didn't leave them.
But they didn't quite stay.

One night, after declining yet another invitation, she sat with her tea and whispered:

"Maybe I didn't lose them. Maybe I just stopped pretending I was okay with the version of me they loved."

That night, her chest didn't feel heavy. Just hollow. And true. The next morning, she made chai without counting cups—just one, hers. The steam rose freely, unhurried by hostess duties. A small rebellion. A quiet homecoming.

Cultural Reflection: The Guilt of Outgrowing

In Indian culture, evolution can feel like rebellion. There's no language for self-trust without disloyalty. If you change, you're accused of forgetting your roots. If you set boundaries, you're called selfish. If you grow spiritually, you're asked why you're "too modern."

There's a cost to being authentic in a culture that rewards endurance over embodiment.

In Gujarati, there's a saying: *"Agar badla, toh bhool gaya."* ("If you changed, it means you forgot us.")

We mistake evolution for erasure—as if honouring your growth means dishonouring their love. As if the river betrays the mountain by flowing onward.

But change isn't forgetting.
It's honouring who you've always been beneath the roles you were praised for.

You're not betraying your people. You're breaking the pattern that silenced them too.

Somatic Insight: The Body's Resistance to Letting Go

Outgrowing isn't just mental. It's cellular.

Your nervous system flinches when you say no—because it remembers the praise that came from saying yes.

Your stomach drops when you leave the group chat—because belonging once meant survival.

Your throat tightens when you decline the call—because silence used to feel like abandonment.

But these are not regressions. They're remnants.
And they will soften.

Final Whisper

Outgrowing doesn't mean you're ungrateful.
It means your spirit chose sunlight over smallness.

You didn't leave anyone behind.
You just walked home to yourself.

Not everyone will follow.
Not everyone should.

But your truth deserves company—even if, at first, it's only your own.

Sacred Reflection

What parts of you have been waiting patiently for permission to grow?
And what old love must you grieve—not because it was false, but because it no longer fits?

✱ Bonus Practice: Science Soothing

Mourning Without Guilt

Some losses don't involve people. They involve old roles — the part of you that used to over-give, over-explain, overstay. This practice is not about cutting cords with cruelty. It's about parting ways with compassion.

✱ Begin by writing a short goodbye letter. Not to the person, but to the version of yourself you became to feel safe. The mask. The performance. Thank it for what it protected. Then release it with a line like, "You helped me survive. But I'm ready to breathe without you now."

✱ When guilt arises — and it will place your hand over your heart.

Let your breath slow. Say gently: "It's okay to miss what I no longer
need." Guilt doesn't mean you're wrong. It often means you're growing.

✱ Now anchor the shift. Name three things that feel more honest since you changed. A boundary you held. A truth you voiced. A silence you honoured. Say each one aloud in front of a mirror. Let your own reflected gaze be the first witness to this becoming.

✱ To close, light a candle. Not for what ended. But for what finally began: you.

Why This Practice Works

Letting go of old roles can trigger guilt because the brain confuses safety with familiarity. Writing a goodbye letter helps the **prefrontal cortex** reframe the story, while mirror-speaking activates **mirror neurons**, reinforcing new identity.

Self-touch and breath calm the **limbic system** by stimulating the **vagus nerve**, helping the body feel safe to change. The candle ritual engages memory and meaning networks — giving the nervous system a symbol that something ended with peace, not threat.

CHAPTER

14

The Echo of What You Didn't Say – How Suppressed Truths Become Symptoms

"What you didn't say didn't disappear. It just took a new shape—in your stomach, your sleep, your silence."

— Dr. Saif Qazi

"The truth has legs. It doesn't stop walking toward you just because you closed the door."

— African Proverb

The Body Knows When You Lie to Yourself

There are things you didn't say. Not because you lied—but because you were taught that silence was survival. Taught to nod instead of name. To appease instead of assert. To keep the peace even if it cost your presence. You learned to trim your voice to fit others' ears—not because you were weak, but because survival once meant making yourself digestible. And your nervous system remembers. It remembers the moment you smiled through discomfort. Laughed when you wanted to leave. Said "it's fine" with a throat full of truths you never got to speak.

But the truth didn't vanish. It settled. In your stomach, as unease. In your throat, as tightness. In your sleep, as restlessness. In your silence, as grief. The nervous system doesn't track social grace—it only tracks safety.

"Speak the truth, even if your voice trembles." — Arab proverb

If the body learns that honesty leads to disconnection, it adapts. It braces. It bites its own tongue. Until one day, it can no longer hold it.

The Biology of Suppressed Speech

Suppressed truths—especially emotional ones—don't simply disappear. Neuroscience shows that inhibition of emotional expression activates the same stress-response circuitry as trauma exposure. The prefrontal cortex suppresses the limbic system to maintain composure, but the cost is cortisol. Muscle tension. Increased heart rate.

Gut dysfunction. Over time, this emotional inhibition becomes the body's baseline.

This is why Arvind's body revolted in silence. Not because he was broken—but because it was the only language left to protest what his voice had been trained to swallow.

The ventral vagal system (social engagement and calm) begins to shut down. The dorsal vagal complex (linked to freeze and shutdown) takes over. You wake up tired. Your jaw aches. You feel heaviness after keeping quiet to "keep the peace."

It's not weakness. It's a body paying interest on truths it was never allowed to spend.

Echo Story: Joshua and the Soundless Years

Joshua, 39, grew up in a joint family where his role was clear: be the reasonable one. The neutraliser. The one who makes things okay. When his parents argued, he played music in the next room. When relatives disrespected him, he smiled. When his heart was broken at 25, he told no one. "Everyone has problems," he'd say.

By 37, he had ulcers that burned like a quiet reproach. His jaw clicked like a locked drawer. His relationships stalled where intimacy began—at the threshold of what went unsaid.

His therapist once asked, "Where does your truth go when you don't say it?"

Arvind blinked. "It goes nowhere. It just… stays."

That year, he began writing letters he'd never send. One to his father. One to a girl who ghosted him. One to himself at age 15. The first time he cried while writing, he vomited. His body wasn't purging sadness—it was releasing the silence.

Sometimes, healing isn't about speaking to others. It's about finally telling the truth within the walls of your own body.

Cultural Reflection: Silence as Survival

In many cultures—especially collectivist ones—truth is filtered through consequences. "If I say this, will I hurt them?" "Will they stop loving me?" "Will I be disloyal?" So we become archivists of the unsaid. We carry ancestral loyalty in our silence. We keep family secrets in our throat. We confuse stillness with strength.

In Marathi, there's a saying: *"सत्य बोलायचं पण सडेतोड नाही."*

(Tell the truth—but don't be too direct.)

But chronic politeness is not compassion. It's often self-abandonment. And what if the kindest thing you can do for your lineage is not to repeat their silence—but to gently exhale what they couldn't?

You are not betraying your family by acknowledging what they could not.
You are not ungrateful for noticing the pain others survived by ignoring.

You are not rude for telling the truth gently.
You are just letting your body breathe again.

The Somatic Cost of the Unspoken

Suppressed truths fossilize in the body—throat stones from swallowed words, stomach acid from unspilled rage, a jaw clenched around all the sentences it never got to speak.

- Tightness in the chest after small betrayals
- Chronic acid reflux after years of "it's fine"
- Fatigue that no amount of rest touches

Dr. Gabor Maté writes, "When we don't say no, our body will say it for us—in symptoms." The body is not punishing you. It's protesting on your behalf.

The Science of Soothing: Giving Voice to the Unspoken

1. Write the Unsent Letter

Pick one person (past or present). Write what you never said. Don't polish it. Don't reread it. Just let it come.

2. Mirror Whisper

Look at yourself in the mirror. Say: *"There is truth inside me. It matters—even if no one hears it."*

3. Somatic Sound

Hum gently with your mouth closed. Let the vibration fill your throat. Feel where the sound meets tension.

4. Safe Release

Speak a sentence out loud that you've never said before. It doesn't need to be dramatic. It just needs to be yours.

5. Breath of Permission

Inhale: *"It's okay to have truth."*

Exhale: *"I'm safe enough to feel it."*

Final Whisper

What you didn't say isn't gone.
It's curled inside your ribs like a second skeleton.
It hums in your throat like a prayer you forgot you memorized.

You don't need to confront anyone.
You just need to stop hiding from the sound of your own truth.

Let your body become a sanctuary where every truth—even the ones that tremble—is allowed to land.

Sacred Reflection

Where in your body does your unsaid truth live?
What's the oldest sentence your body still remembers not saying?
Where does your voice go when you swallow it?
What would it mean to make space for truth—without performance, without apology?
And how might your body soften if you let it finally tell the truth?

✱ Bonus Practice: Science Soothing

Giving Voice to the Unspoken

Some truths were never silenced — they were simply never spoken. This practice invites those words home.

✱ Begin by writing an unsent letter to someone from your past or present. Say what was never said. Don't edit. Don't reread. Let it come through, unfiltered.

✱ Stand before a mirror. Look yourself in the eyes and whisper: "There is truth inside me. It matters — even if no one hears it."

✱ Hum gently with your lips closed. Let the sound vibrate through your throat and chest. Feel where it meets resistance. That tension is not weakness — it's memory.

✱ Speak one sentence aloud that you've never voiced before. It doesn't need to be dramatic. It just needs to be yours.

✱ Close with a breath: Inhale, "It's okay to have truth." Exhale, "I'm safe enough to feel it."

Your truth doesn't have to echo through the world to matter. It just has to echo back to you.

Why This Practice Works

Unspoken emotions often stay stuck in the **limbic system**, activating chronic stress patterns in the body. Writing a letter engages the **prefrontal cortex**, allowing unprocessed emotion to gain structure. Humming stimulates the **vagus nerve**, relaxing the throat and reducing emotional constriction. Speaking aloud activates the **motor-speech pathway**, helping transform internal experience into conscious choice. Over time, this builds emotional fluency — the ability to feel, express, and release.

CHAPTER

15

The Forgotten Language of Safety – Relearning What It Means to Feel Okay

"You spent years learning to survive. Now your body needs to remember how to feel safe without effort."
— Dr. Saif Qazi
"Safety is not the absence of threat—it's the presence of connection."
— Gabor Maté

When Survival Masquerades as Safety

You're calm, but only because you've numbed. You're functional, but always braced. You go through your day on autopilot, mistaking the absence of chaos for the presence of peace.

But real safety doesn't feel like stillness out of fear. It feels like softness without vigilance.

"It's not peace if you had to disappear to achieve it." — Nayyirah Waheed

Many people confuse survival with regulation. They think they're fine because nothing is falling apart. But the truth is: their body is stuck in a subtle freeze. Not activated. Not relaxed. Just suspended.

This is the forgotten language of safety. And your body is ready to remember.

The Nervous System's Map of Familiarity

The nervous system doesn't seek pleasure. It seeks familiarity. If your childhood taught you that being alert equals being loved, or that rest equals weakness, then safety will feel suspicious—and anxiety will feel like home.

According to Dr. Stephen Porges' Polyvagal Theory, our autonomic nervous system scans for threat every few milliseconds. When it detects cues of disconnection, even without overt danger, it shifts into protection mode—fight, flight, freeze, or fawn.

"The body doesn't care if it's safe. It cares if it's known." — Deb Dana

So if hyper-vigilance was your emotional homeland, then stillness will feel foreign. You'll confuse boredom for calm. And when something good finally arrives, your body might say: *This can't be trusted.*

Echo Story: Meenal and the Freeze That Looked Like Strength

Meenal, a 42-year-old school principal in Pune, was known for her grace under pressure. Calm voice. Steady hands. Always "fine."

Her staff said, "She's unshakeable." Her students adored her. But inside, Meenal hadn't felt her heartbeat in years. Not in the way you're supposed to—not as presence, but as panic.

Her father had been emotionally absent. Her mother, perpetually overwhelmed. As a child, she learned: don't cry, don't ask, don't expect. Just keep going.

When her partner of eight years left with barely a goodbye, Meenal didn't fall apart. She made tea. She graded papers. She adjusted the classroom curtains.

It took her therapist six months to help her name what was happening: chronic dorsal vagal freeze. A nervous system stuck in shutdown mode.

"She wasn't calm. She was numb. And numbness wears the costume of resilience. It fools applause into replacing affection."

One day, in the middle of traffic, a rickshaw brushed her car. She trembled—not from fear, but because her body had finally unfrozen.

That's when she knew: she wasn't broken. She had just never been safe enough to feel.

Cultural Reflection: The Myth of Stoic Strength

"When a culture confuses quiet with strong, the body forgets what gentle feels like."

In many South Asian families, emotional silence is praised. Crying is weak. Sensitivity is mocked. Women are expected to endure. Men are told to "be strong."

"Be quiet and carry on" is considered maturity.

We learn to confuse suppression with self-control.

In Tamil, there's a phrase: *"Ullae azhudha udambu thaan sollum."*

("The body tells the story of the tears cried inside.")

Safety, in such homes, is not an embodied state. It is a social role. You perform stability. You wear silence. You function on a borrowed nervous system.

But no matter how well you play the part, your body always remembers the unsaid.

Neuroscience of Relearning Safety

"You can't think your way into feeling safe. You have to feel your way there—one cue at a time."

The good news: the nervous system is neuroplastic. With consistent cues of connection, it can rewire its default settings.

Dr. Daniel Siegel explains that "co-regulation precedes self-regulation." You don't regulate in isolation. You regulate through safe others—through felt presence, not logical reasoning.

You don't calm yourself by saying "I'm safe." You calm yourself when your body starts to believe it.

This means healing isn't about affirmations. It's about experience.

"Safety is not a mantra. It's a muscle memory." — Dr. Nicole LePera

The vagus nerve, your body's main communicator between brain and gut, responds to tone, breath, and micro-cues of safety. Eye contact. Gentle voice. Rhythm. Stillness. These are the things that slowly convince the body to come home.

Final Whisper

You don't have to wait for a breakdown to begin remembering safety.
You don't need a diagnosis to deserve softness.

Your body is not broken.
It just speaks the language of yesterday.

And it is ready to learn a gentler one.

Not all healing is dramatic. Some of it looks like this:
A full breath.
A loosening jaw.
A moment where nothing bad happens, and the body finally notices

What does safety feel like in your body—not in theory, but in sensation?
Who or what reminds your nervous system that it doesn't have to brace?
And what would it mean to let safety become your new first language?

✱ Bonus Practice: Science Soothing

Relearning the Language

These aren't fixes. They are invitations — soft doorways back to the parts of you that were never broken, only buried.

✱ Begin with a grounded scan. Sit quietly. Feel your feet. Your seat. The air around you. Whisper: "This is now. This is safe." Let this be a visit, not a verdict.

✱ Record yourself reading a gentle line like: "You don't have to brace anymore." Play it back once a day. This isn't reprogramming. It's reintroducing your body to the sound of safety — in your own voice.

✱ Practice the exhale anchor: Inhale for four counts. Exhale for eight. Not to force calm — but to tell your nervous system: "We're not rushing. We're allowed to exist here."

✱ Create a co-regulation list — names, songs, scents, animals that remind your body of warmth. Use the list like a window, not an escape. Let it remind you that connection doesn't have to be earned.

* Finally, lie down for ten minutes in the middle of your day. Not to recharge. Not to prove anything. Just to rehearse what it feels like to be — without performing.

Let each practice be a gesture of reunion, not correction.

Why This Practice Works

Trauma and chronic stress can cause the brain to associate stillness with danger and rest with guilt. The **insula** and **default mode network** play key roles in self-awareness and emotional identity — these practices reawaken both, gently. Slow exhales activate the **parasympathetic nervous system**, grounding the body in present safety. Hearing your own voice with compassionate words strengthens **auditory-limbic loops**, helping replace internal criticism with care. Each repetition teaches your nervous system a new language: not of control, but of quiet permission.

CHAPTER 16

The Body as Proof – How Healing Shows Up Without Needing to Be Announced

"Your body doesn't wait for language. It keeps score. And it also keeps record of every soft return."
— Dr. Saif Qazi

"We are healed not when we're fixed, but when we're felt—in our own skin."
— Somatic wisdom proverb

The Proof No One Applauds

You didn't post about it. No before-and-after photos. No triumphant captions. Just this: your hand resting on your chest without prompting, like it finally recognized home. You exhaled without being told to. You laughed—not for performance, but from the belly. You paused before reacting. You noticed your jaw wasn't clenched.

That was healing.

Not a breakthrough. Not a transformation. Just a quiet, physiological shift that whispered rather than announced itself. You didn't earn it. You didn't schedule it. You didn't even expect it. But your body gave it to you anyway—as if to say: *we're safe enough now.*

We are taught to think healing looks like milestones: confronting your past, changing your life, forgiving everyone, announcing your peace. But the real markers are subtler. They live inside the body, not on a timeline.

Sometimes healing looks like the breath you didn't realise you were holding. The walk you took without checking your phone. The silence that didn't scare you. The moment your nervous system didn't flinch—even when it used to.

"Healing doesn't always roar. Sometimes, it exhales."

Healing is not when your pain is gone. It's when your body stops bracing for it.

"You will not attain wholeness until you listen to the body's wisdom." — Abu Zayd al-Balkhi *(9th-century Islamic psychologist)*

The Science of Internal Safety

The human body holds an ancient wisdom that rarely needs permission to speak—but often needs safety to be heard. At the heart of this is *interoception*—your internal sense of how things are going within. It includes the awareness of your heartbeat, the rhythm of your breath, your body temperature, digestion, and muscular tension.

Neuroscientist Bud Craig refers to interoception as the *root of all emotion.*

When your nervous system is dysregulated, interoception is distorted. You may become hypervigilant—sensing too much, too often—or you go numb, sensing nothing at all. Trauma doesn't just create fear. It confuses the body's ability to read itself.

"Safety is not calmness—it's the absence of pretense." — *Dr. Saif Qazi*

When interoception heals, the body stops filing injury reports—Rebecca's unexpected second exhale wasn't magic. It was her vagus nerve finally trusting daylight.

You know you're healing not because your mind says, "I'm okay," but because your body stops asking: *Are we still in danger?*

It's when:

- You stop negotiating with your own breath.
- Stillness doesn't feel like threat.
- Hunger feels like hunger—not shame.
- Movement becomes play—not penance.

These aren't spiritual awakenings. They are biological reconciliations.

Echo Story: Rebecca and the Second Exhale

Rebecca, 38, had done all the work. Inner child therapy. Journaling. Breathwork. She could name her triggers. Quote every expert. Teach the language of healing fluently. But she hadn't rested in months.

Each morning, she rose with a mission. To be healed. To be better. To finally be done with the ache. She tracked her nervous system like a report card. Her body was exhausted by the performance of wellness.

Then one day, while watering her balcony plants, she noticed the basil leaves trembling in the morning air. She stood still—not to meditate, not to ground—but simply because her body stopped moving. No insight arrived. No mantra came. She inhaled. And then—unexpectedly—she exhaled again.

It was the second exhale that changed everything. The one that wasn't planned. The one her body gave her freely. No reward. No permission. Just release.

Later, she noticed her slippers still on, her tea gone cold—ordinary things that would have irritated her before. Now they were just evidence: she had been elsewhere. Present.

"The body never lies. It just waits for permission to speak again."

Rebecca realised: healing wasn't something she needed to orchestrate. It was something her body had already begun returning to—quietly, patiently, breath by breath.

Cultural Reflection: Healing Without Proving

In many cultures, healing is expected to be visible. "Show us how far you've come." "Let us see how much you've changed." Recovery becomes a pageant. Transformation is measured in productivity, detachment, and radiance.

But true healing doesn't perform. Sometimes it looks like cancelled plans. Like saying "I don't know." Like sleeping all weekend and not apologising for it. Sometimes healing looks like the exact opposite of what people expect.

In Urdu, there's a line: *"Sukoon dikhta nahi, mehsoos hota hai."* (Peace doesn't show—it is felt.)

We treat recovery like a wedding—something to be seen, photographed, celebrated on schedule. But grief and grace are monsoon rains: they arrive when they will, and the earth knows better than to demand an explanation.

Let your nervous system be the only witness. Let your proof be private. Let your body hum its quiet songs without needing applause.

"When you heal for yourself, not your image, the body thanks you in languages you forgot you spoke."

You do not need to convince anyone you're okay.
You only need to notice when your body stops asking for permission to exist.

Somatic Insight: The Body's Healing Signals

What does healing feel like when it arrives quietly, through the skin?

It's the jaw that softens halfway through the day.
The breath that drops into your belly without prompting.
The tears that come without shame.
The stomach that stops clenching before a phone call.
The spine that straightens—not in defence, but in dignity.
The way your toes uncurl in sleep.
The yawn that arrives not from tiredness, but surrender.
The absent-minded hum your throat remembers from childhood.

The nervous system is polyphonic—it doesn't declare change. It hums it. And if you listen carefully, you'll notice:

"You won't always feel like a new person. Sometimes you'll just feel more like yourself."

Final Whisper

You don't need to shout your healing.
You don't need to perform your peace.

The proof is already here:

- In the space between your breaths.
- In the unclenching.
- In the way your body no longer startles at ease.

You are the proof.
And your body remembers.

Sacred Reflection

What signs of healing has your body shown you lately—so quietly you almost missed them?
What would it feel like to let peace be private?
And who would you be if you didn't have to explain how far you've come—only feel it?

✱ Bonus Practice: Science Soothing

The Proof Practice – Letting the Body Speak First

✱ Pause and wait for the second exhale. Let it come without force. That's your body saying, *"I feel safe enough now."*

✱ Soften your jaw mid-day. No ritual. Just awareness. Let go of what you're holding unconsciously.

✱ Sit still for two minutes. Not to ground. Just to be. If silence feels okay, that's healing.

✱ Place your hand on your heart. Whisper: *"You've made it through another day."* Let your body hear it without needing a

reason.

Why This Practice Works

These subtle acts strengthen **interoception**—your body's ability to feel itself. The second exhale, jaw release, and stillness all signal a shift from vigilance to safety. Gentle self-touch activates the **vagus nerve**, calming the **limbic system** and reinforcing internal trust. Healing isn't always dramatic—it's the body recognising it no longer needs to brace.

PART FOUR

Becoming Your Own Sanctuary

CHAPTER

17

The New Normal – Learning to Live Without Waiting for the Other Shoe to Drop

The Confusing Calm

You've spent so many years bracing for storms that when the sky finally clears, you don't trust the blue—you search for the seam where the clouds might return.

"The moon is most beautiful when it's not watched." — Japanese Zen proverb

Calm doesn't feel like freedom; it feels like unfamiliar ground. Your nervous system, trained to flinch at every shift in weather, keeps scanning the sky, just in case. Even joy comes with suspicion. Even softness feels like a setup.

This isn't because you're broken. It's because your body learned to survive, not to rest. And now that the war is over, the soldier in you doesn't know where to put down the armour.

"When you've lived in a storm long enough, even sunlight feels like a warning."

Vihaan's Story: Suspicious of Stability

Vihaan, a backend engineer from Chennai, had finally secured the job he used to pray for. Remote. Safe. Fair pay. But each time he opened his laptop, he expected to be let go. When his manager praised him, he rehearsed disaster. At night, he'd lie awake, tracing the cracks in his bedroom ceiling like they were fault lines—waiting for the tremor that never came.

In therapy, he whispered, "It's like my body is addicted to panic. I can't stop waiting for something to go wrong."

He wasn't resisting success. He was protecting himself from the cost he had always associated with joy.

"Peace felt like borrowed time. Calm felt like a test. Joy felt like betrayal."

How the Brain Misreads Peace

Your amygdala, the brain's internal alarm bell, doesn't ask, "Is this moment joyful?" It asks, "Is this familiar?"

And if chaos was your normal, then stability will feel like a foreign language—beautiful, but untrustworthy.

A study at the University of British Columbia found that people raised in unpredictable environments develop "anticipatory threat loops," where even calm moments trigger low-level stress. The body, confused by unfamiliar safety, stays on alert. That's not pessimism. That's protection.

But your brain can change. Neuroplasticity allows us to create new emotional baselines—not by force, but by gentle, consistent repetition.

"Your nervous system doesn't need more proof of danger. It needs new memories of peace."

Cultural Legacy: The Inherited Alarm

In many Indian homes, hyper-awareness was passed down like heirloom silver—polished by worry, weighted with warning. We were taught not to relax too much, not to laugh too loudly, not to trust joy without consequence. Joy was seen as arrogant. Rest was indulgent. Safety was temporary.

These weren't superstitions. They were inherited grief rituals—echoes of lives shaped by partition, poverty, loss. We learned to carry vigilance in our bones, not because we were ungrateful—but because our ancestors couldn't afford to be caught off guard.

But you are not betraying them by choosing calm. You are fulfilling their dream: that one day, someone would be safe enough to stop looking over their shoulder.

"Your ancestors didn't survive so you could keep suffering. They survived so one day, you wouldn't have to."

Healing Without Bracing

Letting go of your survival script doesn't mean dishonouring it. It means recognizing it did its job—and that now, you need a new story. One where good things don't need to be pre-paid; where joy doesn't come with a disclaimer; where you're allowed to feel okay without checking the emotional weather forecast every five minutes. Some days you'll still brace. That's okay. But now, you'll notice it. And whisper gently: *This is not then. I am safe now.*

"You are no longer living in a battlefield. You can stop acting like you might be ambushed at any moment.

The Final Turn: Letting Life Happen Without Fear

There is no other shoe. No hidden invoice. No debt to pay for this peace. You are allowed to feel good without it being a trick. You are allowed to belong to this new softness without needing a backup plan.

This is not denial. It's reclamation.

"You weren't born to stay alert forever. You were born to rest, to receive, to return."

Sacred Reflection

If peace no longer needed to be justified, what part of your life would

you finally allow yourself to enjoy?

✱ Bonus Practice: Science Soothing

Rehearsing a New Rhythm

Let your healing become a rhythm—not a breakthrough. Each night, write down three quiet moments of safety:

✱ A moment that didn't need fixing

✱ A smile that felt effortless

✱ A task completed without panic

Not as a gratitude list, but as a nervous system rehearsal. A reminder: *"Nothing collapsed. I am allowed to rest."*

"You don't need to fight for every breath anymore. You get to keep it."

Why This Practice Works

Your nervous system learns through repetition. Noticing safe, uneventful moments activates the **prefrontal cortex**, helping reframe daily life as non-threatening. Recording these signals builds emotional memory, while the act of reflection reduces cortisol and activates the **parasympathetic response**. Over time, your body begins to trust stillness—not just endure it.

CHAPTER

18

Becoming the Safe Place You Sought – Healing as a Living Practice

The Shift from Survival to Sanctuary

Healing isn't a single event. It's not a milestone you cross with fanfare or a moment where everything suddenly feels better. It's not even about erasing your past. Healing is the slow, tender process of building a home inside yourself that doesn't collapse when fear knocks. It is not the absence of pain—it is the presence of safety. Not the removal of fear—but the return of trust.

You spent years searching for safety in others. In lovers, in mentors, in the validation of strangers. And often, they gave you pieces of it. But it never lasted, did it? Because the deepest safety isn't external. It's internal.

"You are not a drop in the ocean. You are the entire ocean in a drop." — Rumi

It's the soft, steady knowing that no matter what breaks outside, you won't abandon yourself again.

"You were never just seeking love. You were seeking a home that wouldn't disappear when you finally arrived."

Mariya's Story: Becoming Her Own Shelter

Mariya, a young architect from Kolkata, had always apologised for her presence. She tiptoed around others' moods, diluted her joy, and translated her needs into silence. Her childhood taught her that emotions were burdens, not signals. That the less she needed, the more she would be accepted.

Her voice would tremble when setting boundaries, as if her throat remembered generations of silencing. One evening, after yet another conflict where she kept herself small to keep the peace, she asked herself: "What if I treated myself like someone I'd promised to protect?"

She began a ritual. A candle lit before hard conversations. A journal prompt before sleep: *What would safety look like tonight?* A small note on her mirror: *You're allowed to take up space.*

Over time, she didn't just feel better. She felt *safer* — not because the world changed, but because she did.

"When the world couldn't hold her gently, she learned to hold herself."

The Neuroscience of Self-Safety

The body doesn't know the difference between external comfort and internal reassurance—it only knows signals. When you speak kindly to yourself, when you slow your breath, when you soothe your own panic without shame—you activate the vagus nerve. This sends a message across your body: "You are not in danger."

Research at Yale's Centre for Emotional Intelligence confirms this. Regular self-validation practices reduce cortisol and increase emotional resilience.

That means talking to yourself with gentleness isn't corny. It's biochemical healing. That means placing a hand on your heart isn't dramatic. It's a nervous system recalibration. Your body listens to your tone even when your mind doesn't believe your words—yet.

"You don't heal by becoming harder. You heal by becoming safer to come home to."

Dev and the Inner Mentor

Dev, a 43-year-old schoolteacher from Assam, had spent most of his life playing the strong one. Supporting a widowed mother. Guiding younger siblings. Carrying his family's expectations like sacred weight.

When he finally moved to a new city to chase his quiet dream of writing, guilt followed like a shadow. He had never practised choosing himself. Every joyful moment felt like a betrayal.

A friend once told him: "When you're unsure, ask: what would I tell my son in this situation?"

Dev began writing letters from his future self—ones that didn't scold, but encouraged. One note read: *You are not selfish for choosing joy. You are simply breaking the rule that love must always come last.* He became his own elder. His own guide. His own safe place.

"Sometimes healing is not becoming someone new. It's finally becoming someone kind."

Cultural Conditioning: The Confusion Between Care and Control

In Indian homes, care often came wrapped in control. Love was expressed through warnings. Protection was spoken in scolding. The message was: "We care for you—so we get to decide for you."

"Don't wear that—people will talk."
"Don't laugh so loudly in front of guests."
"We love you—so we know what's best for you."

And so, many of us grew up confusing restriction with affection. We didn't learn autonomy—we learned adaptation. We learned to earn safety by becoming smaller, quieter, easier to manage.

But true healing doesn't ask you to shrink. It asks you to remember that you were never too much. You were just too unprotected.

"You weren't hard to love. You were just taught that love should hurt a little."

The Final Turn

You searched for someone to come sit with you in the dark. But the miracle is this: it was always you. Your presence. Your tenderness. Your noticing.

You are no longer a guest in your own nervous system. You are the architect now. You can build softness where harshness once lived. You can lay down the armour. You can light the lamp—not for illumination, but to remind your body that the dark is no longer danger.

"You are not waiting for home. You are becoming it."

Sacred Reflection

If you treated your inner world like sacred ground, how would you speak to yourself when no one is listening.

✱ Bonus Practice: Science Soothing

Build an Inner Safe Space

Think of a recent moment you felt overwhelmed or unsafe. Don't analyse it—just name it.

Light a candle or touch the space between your collarbones. Let this simple ritual say: *"I'm here. You're not alone."*

Now speak to yourself like someone you'd never abandon: *"I see you. You're allowed to feel this. I'm not going anywhere."*

Place a hand over your heart. Let your body absorb it not as an idea, but as an experience. Do this often. This is not drama. This is rehearsal.

"When safety becomes familiar, you no longer chase it. You carry it."

Why This Practice Works

Emotional overwhelm activates the **amygdala**, making the body feel

under threat. Interrupting it with ritual engages the **sensory nervous system**, helping ground you in the present. Touching the chest or collarbone stimulates the **vagus nerve**, shifting the body into a parasympathetic state. When paired with soothing self-talk, this builds **emotional muscle memory**—so safety becomes a state you return to, not something you seek outside.

CHAPTER 19

The Quiet Power of Staying – How Consistency Becomes Your New Superpower

"Healing isn't a lightning bolt. It's the thousandth morning you choose your own presence over the drama of departure."
— Dr. Saif Qazi
"The slowest transformation is often the most permanent."
— Somatic Wisdom

The Sacredness of Showing Up Again

You stretch your spine before checking your phone. You listen to the quiet before asking the world what it needs from you. You stay.

This is the kind of power that doesn't perform. It hums. It settles. It rewires. It whispers to your nervous system: *"You are safe enough to begin again."*

In a world addicted to novelty and speed, staying is an act of rebellion. Especially for those whose nervous systems were shaped by chaos. If your past taught you to brace for the next rupture, then consistency isn't natural—it's revolutionary. It tells your brain, *this time is different.* It tells your body, *we're not leaving.*

The slow return becomes its own ceremony. Not flashy. Not cinematic. But deeply embodied.

Staying doesn't mean clinging. It means returning—to breath, to practice, to presence—without needing to start over. Again and again.

"Regularity, when rightly practiced, becomes a form of devotion." — Swami Vivekananda

Because the most sacred transformation isn't in arriving somewhere new. It's in discovering you already belong here, and choosing to stay anyway.

Echo Story: Isha and the Repatterned Mornings

Isha had tried everything. Somatic therapy. Meditation. Journaling. She'd healed in bursts—powerful retreats, intense catharsis, moments of pure clarity. But her life still felt like a cycle: breakthrough, burnout, begin again.

What changed wasn't a miracle. It was a Monday.

She decided to stop chasing peak states. Instead, she made cardamom tea at 7:03 a.m., letting the steam fog the window where the sun hit first. No affirmations. No metrics. Just the heat of the cup, the slant of light, and her breath learning to trust the ordinary.

At first, it felt meaningless. But two months later, her therapist asked, "Do you still feel like you're starting from scratch every week?"

She smiled. "No. I think I finally built something that doesn't collapse when life gets loud."

The transformation didn't come from intensity. It came from repetition. From the nervous system learning that safety wasn't a performance—but a pattern.

✦ Why Repetition Heals: The Neuroscience of Consistency

Your brain doesn't rewire through intensity—it rewires through repetition. Neuroplasticity, the brain's lifelong ability to form new connections, is not activated by one-time shifts, but by rhythmic exposure. Every time you repeat a calming behaviour—whether it's five slow breaths, a gentle stretch, or sitting in silence at the same window—you signal safety to the nervous system. That cue becomes a thread. Repeat it often enough, and it becomes a new neural path. Eventually, a new baseline.

Dr. Andrew Huberman emphasises that it's not the length of time you spend in a new state that alters your physiology—it's the frequency with which you revisit it. Frequency builds familiarity. Familiarity builds trust. And trust becomes the new floor beneath your emotional life.

For trauma survivors, repetition is like rebuilding a bridge while walking it. At first, each step feels tentative—will it hold? But with time, the body learns: this path won't vanish beneath me.

When you've lived through emotional inconsistency, your nervous system learns to brace. You become fluent in chaos and suspicious of peace. But repetition—gentle, predictable, kind—tells your brain a new story: "I am safe here, and I will be safe tomorrow too."

This is why staying is a healing superpower. It builds coherence in a world that taught you fragmentation. It makes your internal world easier to return to—because it becomes inhabitable. Not perfect, not always regulated, but familiar in the best way.

Consistency isn't discipline. It's loyalty—to your breath, to your pauses, to the version of you that no longer begs for permission to rest.

Cultural Reflection: Reclaiming Loyalty to Self

Many of us were taught loyalty as sacrifice. Loyalty to family. To duty. To roles that eroded us. But rarely were we taught to be loyal to *ourselves*—to routines that nourish us, to rituals that keep us rooted.

In South Asian culture, repetition is often linked with devotion—chants, diya lighting, sacred routines. What if healing used that same rhythm? What if your nervous system is not asking for another breakthrough—but a gentle ritual to return to each day? What if your first breath at dawn is your new zikr, each cycle of breath whispering La ilaha illallah as the Sufis have done for centuries?

'Wherever you stand, be the soul of that place,' Rumi advises

What if your morning ritual became that sacred grounding? The ritual isn't just about devotion to something beyond you—but to the self that's always been worthy of return, the way a whirling dervish returns to his axis with every turn, the way the moon returns to fullness after every waning.

To stay isn't stagnation. It's the quiet rebellion of roots—refusing to uproot yourself just to prove you can grow elsewhere.

"To stay is to tell your younger self: I won't leave you this time."

Final Whisper

Staying rarely roars.
It's the quiet hum of a kettle at dawn.
The uncelebrated act of tying your shoelaces when no one's watching.
The way roots grow—not with fanfare, but with fidelity to the dark.
But each return rewrites the nervous system's story.
Not abandoned. Not rushed. Not betrayed.

Just this:
You stayed.

And slowly, the body starts believing:
We are no longer leaving ourselves behind.

Sacred Reflection

What have you been tempted to abandon that's actually helping you heal?
What would it mean to return—not dramatically, but quietly?
What rhythm might become your new resilience if you let it repeat?
What's the 'ordinary' ritual that's secretly holding you together?
Where has leaving yourself become a habit—and what would staying look like there?

✱ Bonus Practice: Science Soothing

Rehearsing the Return
Choose one grounding ritual—light a candle, hum, step outside barefoot. Do it at the same time each day. Keep it under five minutes. Let it be enough.

Each day, note one thing that felt safe—a soft silence, a shared glance, a breath that didn't rush. Write it down. Repetition builds body memory.

Each night, whisper: *"I showed up today."* Let it mean everything. You're not here to impress the world. You're here to keep meeting yourself.

Place your hand over your chest and say: *"I am learning to stay—with myself, not just for others."*

And when you skip a day, return without punishment. Healing isn't perfection. It's pattern.

"The moon returns. The river returns. You, darling, are allowed to come home to yourself a thousand times."
— *Rumi*

Why This Practice Works

The nervous system thrives on rhythm. Anchoring a daily ritual supports **neuroplasticity**, helping the brain encode new patterns of safety. Naming a felt-safe moment activates the **hippocampus**, reinforcing emotional recall linked to calm.

Simple affirmations paired with touch stimulate the **vagus nerve**,
grounding your system in self-attunement. And when you return without shame, you rewire the **anterior cingulate cortex**, reducing self-judgment and restoring emotional resilience.

Returning is not failure. It's fidelity to growth.

CHAPTER

20

The Return to Yourself – You Were Never Broken, Only Buried

The Myth of Reinvention

You were told healing would sculpt you into something else—shinier, sharper, a version of you with the messy parts sanded down. But true healing doesn't sand. It uncovers.

True healing doesn't make you unrecognisable. It makes you *unapologetically familiar.*

"He who has not found his own self cannot find anything else." — Maulana Jalaluddin Rumi

You don't become someone else. You become someone you once abandoned—and now remember.

You were never broken. You were only buried—under borrowed stories, under shame that wasn't yours to carry, under roles that fit like someone else's skin.

"You are not a project. You are a return."

Why Coming Home Feels Like Grief

Most people expect transformation to feel like a sunrise.

But sometimes, it feels like mourning. Because to become who you truly are, you must let go of who you became to survive.

That self—the achiever, the pleaser, the silent one, the fighter—deserves gratitude, not shame. They carried you through. But they cannot take you further.

"Healing is not about fixing what is wrong with you. It is about grieving who you had to be."

Aanchal's Homecoming

Aanchal, a quiet artist from Delhi, spent years trying to become better. More productive. More pleasing. More resilient. Her notebooks were filled with affirmations and improvement plans.

But one rainy evening, she found a poem she had written at age nine:

"I am enough even when the stars don't notice."

The paper smelled of monsoon damp and pencil lead. The "e" in "enough" was dotted with a tiny heart.

She wept. Not because it was beautiful. But because it was *true.*

That small voice—the one that once dared to feel enough—had waited patiently beneath years of edits, deadlines, and diminishing returns.

That child had known something the adult forgot: worth is not a wage paid in exhaustion. It is remembered through softness.

From that night, she stopped writing to prove. She began writing to feel. To return. To create without contortion.

"The self you buried for survival is still waiting where you left her. Whole. Breathing. Ready."

The Science of Remembering

Neuroplasticity isn't just about new pathways—it's about rewilding old ones. The neural trails where you once knew play, trust, asking—grown over but not gone.

When the body is no longer rehearsing collapse, it begins reaching for curiosity again—breath deepens, muscles soften, trust rewires.

You don't just evolve forward. You *reclaim backward.*

That is what healing is: memory returning to the body.

"Your wholeness isn't a future goal. It is a past truth waiting to be re-invited."

Cultural Reframing: Evolution Without Betrayal

In many cultures, softening is mistaken for weakness. Changing your mind is equated with instability. Choosing peace is seen as abandoning tradition.

But evolution is not disloyalty.

You are not cutting your roots by growing—you're proving they're still alive. Your ancestors did not survive their storms so you could inherit only their fear. They endured so that someone—maybe you—could feel what they never dared to.

You are not here to burn everything down. You are here to grow things they never had the chance to.

"Healing is not rebellion. It is rooted remembrance."

The Final Whisper

You don't need more effort.
You need more remembering.
You don't need to become.
You need to return.

You don't need to perform. You need to pause.
You don't need to prove. You just need to feel—and stay.

You were never meant to be a masterpiece built by others. You are the masterpiece—not under restoration, just under layers of dust.

"Come home. The door has been open all along."

Sacred Reflection

If you knew you were never broken, what would you finally allow yourself to receive, create, or become?

✱ Bonus Practice: Science Soothing

The Homecoming Letter

Light a candle. Let its glow be the first to welcome you home.

Close your eyes and picture the version of you that existed before fear took the lead.
What did they love?
What felt like truth?
What did they still believe was possible?

Now write to them. Welcome them back. Apologise for the silence. Promise to stay.

This is not self-help. It's self-reunion.
You are not erasing the past — you're inviting the truest parts of you forward.

"The reunion begins the moment you stop hiding from your own eyes."

Why This Practice Works

Writing to a younger or unguarded version of yourself activates the **default mode network (DMN)**—the part of your brain responsible for self-reflection, personal memory, and identity integration. It allows your mind to gently revisit old emotional imprints without reliving them in crisis.

When you pair letter-writing with visualisation (e.g., imagining your past self) and symbolic sensory input (like candlelight), you stimulate both **cognitive reappraisal** and **emotional regulation circuits**. The **medial prefrontal cortex** helps you reflect without shame, while the **anterior cingulate cortex** reduces internal conflict between who you were and who you are becoming.

Placing your attention on safety, forgiveness, and reconnection signals your **ventral vagal system**, which downregulates hyperarousal in the **limbic brain**. Over time, this builds **internal co-regulation** — the ability to offer comfort to yourself without external validation.

This is not just emotional work. It's deep neurobiological integration — where memory meets compassion and identity becomes whole again.

Acknowledgments

Books are not written by individuals.
They are carried by invisible hands
the ones who loved you, challenged you, and stayed when you forgot your own worth.

To the readers holding these pages:
Thank you for trusting me with your time, your hopes, and your hidden chapters.
May you find in these words a reflection of your own quiet power.
To my teachers, mentors, and every soul who walked ahead of me lighting torches when I only knew darkness:
Your courage built the paths I now invite others to walk.

To the people who challenged me, misunderstood me, or left me:
You gave me the resilience to know that validation is not necessary for truth to survive.
To my family:
For your sacrifices, your dreams, and the silent ways you taught me endurance.
This book is stitched from threads you helped weave.
And to the parts of myself I once abandoned:
Thank you for waiting patiently.
This is for all of us—
still learning, still returning, still becoming.

With humility and hope,
Dr. Saif Qazi

Closing Note

A Soft Goodbye – and a Powerful Beginning

Dear Reader,

If you have travelled with me until this page,
then you already know—

Healing isn't a single sunrise.
It's a quiet, stubborn devotion to yourself.

There were moments in this journey that asked you to pause.
Moments that asked you to grieve.
Moments that asked you to stretch into uncomfortable truths.

And you stayed.

That staying—
that gentle refusal to abandon yourself again—
is more powerful than any promise this world could offer you.

You have touched the edges of old pain.
You have reclaimed parts of yourself you once buried for safety.

You have remembered that you are not a broken project—
You are a living, breathing, evolving masterpiece.

This is not the end of your journey.

It is the first true beginning.

- A life built not on survival reflexes—
  but on conscious choosing.
- A life where safety is an inside job.
- A life where belonging starts at home—inside your own chest.

You are allowed to grow slowly.
You are allowed to stumble with grace.
You are allowed to build a life that feels like a sanctuary.

There will be days ahead when the old voices whisper again.
When fear knocks again.
When exhaustion tempts you to forget.

But now, you know:

You can answer those voices not with shame—
but with kindness.

You can meet the mirror not with judgment—
but with welcome.

You can walk into uncertainty not as a victim—
but as a creator.

You are no longer seeking permission to exist.

You are here.
You are whole.
You are enough.

Exactly as you are.
And infinitely more than you ever believed.

From my heart to yours,
thank you for trusting me to walk beside you.
Even if only for a few pages of your life.

May you keep choosing yourself,
over and over again,
until it no longer feels like a rebellion—
but like breathing.

With quiet faith in you,
Dr. Saif Qazi

About the Author

Dr. Saif Qazi is a family physician, Rotarian, and social reformer dedicated to the intersection of science, service, and self-remembrance.

With over fifteen years of experience in medicine and integrative wellness, he has witnessed first-hand that healing is never just about treating the body—it is about restoring the mind's clarity, the heart's courage, and the spirit's quiet strength.

As a committed Rotarian and advocate for social uplift, Dr. Saif works tirelessly to create real-world change through health initiatives, education, and community development.

His writing bridges worlds—where emotional truth meets biological wisdom, and where practical strategies meet compassionate reflection.

When he's not guiding others toward their own return, he continues to serve communities, nurture resilience, and champion the dignity and potential of every individual he encounters.

This is his invitation to you:
To stop chasing new versions of yourself—
and to start trusting the one that has always been waiting.

Say Hello

hello@drsaifqazi.in

www.drsaifqazi.in

Also by the Author: Reprogram

While Alive Beneath the Ashes explores healing through immersive stories and deep emotional reflection, Reprogram is its poetic twin. It is written for readers who seek soul-shifting clarity through fewer words and deeper silences.

Both books uncover the same truth: you are not broken, only wired by survival. Alive Beneath the Ashes walks beside you like a compassionate guide, while Reprogram acts as a mirror that reflects your inner world.

Written in the lyrical MirrorVerse™ style, Reprogram blends neuroscience, identity, and transformation into a compact, powerful experience.

It is perfect for those who want a meditative journey that speaks to the subconscious and heals through resonance, not effort.

📒 *Now available globally in paperback and digital formats.*

📒 Read it when you're ready to return to yourself.

9 789334 295009